Happy B'day Paul!
The
p...
12/20/03

DEDICATION

To my grandson, Dylan:

May life always bring you the unending joy
you have brought to our family.
You are truly a gift from God.

Love,
Your Bayla

Series Created By • Beverly Cohn
Designers • Peter Hess & Marguerite Jones
Research • Laurie Cohn

Special thanks to Kenny Bookbinder for his invaluable help with the Sports section.

CONTENTS

PRESIDENT KENNEDY'S CIVIL RIGHTS SPEECH

66 Fires of frustration and discord are burning in every city, north and south. Where legal remedies are not at hand, redress is sought in the streets, in demonstrations, parades and protests, which create tensions and threaten violence and threaten lives. We face, therefore, a moral crisis as a country and a people. We have a right to expect that the Negro community will be responsible, will uphold the law. But they have a right to expect that the law will be fair – that the Constitution will be color blind as Justice Harlan said at the turn of the century. This is what we're talking about and this is the matter which concerns this country and what it stands for and in meeting it, I ask the support of all of our citizens. Thank you very much. **99**

1963 Civil Rights March

Arriving by train, by bus and by air from all parts of the country, they come united in one cause – to urge Congress to pass a civil rights bill to end forever the blight of racial inequity.

This great throng gathers on the Mall that stretches from the Washington Monument toward the Capitol.

By 9:30 a.m. it is estimated that 40,000 people have assembled. But it's more like a Sunday outing as they form into groups and discuss the day quietly. Few realize that they are participants in a historical day; that today's gathering is the largest in Washington's history.

WHAT A YEAR IT WAS!

in Washington, D.C.  1963

Just 100 years after Lincoln signed the Emancipation Proclamation that freed the slaves, 200,000 people converge on the nation's capital to rally for civil rights.

The men who organized the rally walk toward the speaker's stand. Roy Wilkins (*inset, left*) walks with A. Philip Randolph. They have fought this fight all of their adult lives.

Martin Luther King, Jr. (*left*), who has been jailed 12 times on racial issues, marches as does Walter Reuther (*right*), head of the Auto Workers.

Authorities are fearful of disorder and there are 4,000 uniformed men on duty. Actually, arrests in Washington are below normal and police attribute this to the fact that for the first time in 30 years you couldn't buy even a beer in Washington. The marchers sing songs ranging from sacred to hillbilly, but with the one recurring theme: the cause of 20 million blacks.

The crowd assembles around the Reflecting Pool in front

of the Lincoln Memorial, occupying every inch on the lawns and under the trees.

There is a great swell of cheers to welcome Martin Luther King, Jr., to the speaker's podium, who transforms the day from an outing to a crusade. *"I still have a dream. It is a dream chiefly rooted in the American dream. I have a dream that one day this nation will rise up and live out the true meaning of its creed: 'We hold these truths to be self-evident, that all men are created equal.' I have a dream."* Rev. King stands as a symbol of all they are fighting for.

1963 VIETNAMESE AND COM

Tanks ring Buddhist temples in Vietnam as the crisis in that embattled Southeast Asian nation mounts to a climax.

These troops are under the command of Ngo Dinh Nhu, the president's brother.

The next step by Nhu is the wholesale arrest of college students sympathetic to the cause of the Buddhists.

BUDDHIST
MUNIST CRISIS

1963

Following a roundup of Buddhist monks, Ngo Dinh Nhu sends a demand to Ambassador Henry Cabot Lodge that he hand over monks who have taken refuge in the American embassy, which the ambassador refuses to do.

The bitter strife between Buddhists and the government comes in the midst of Vietnam's fight against Communist rebels. The Buddhists, demanding more religious freedom, find themselves the object of a terror campaign that has had international repercussions. The U.S. has poured 14,000 advisors and $3 billion into Vietnam and subsequently advises President Ngo Dinh Diem to remove his brother from office.

Protesting South Vietnam's President Ngo Dinh's persecution of Buddhists, 17-year-old monk Ngo Quang Duc dies by self-immolation.

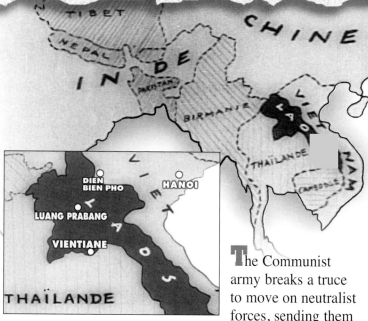

Units of the Seventh Fleet on patrol in the South China Sea and Laos and Vietnam are put on the alert as the situation in Laos continues to mount to a new crisis.

The Communist army breaks a truce to move on neutralist forces, sending them reeling back. Then comes another ceasefire, but the situation is a grave one and President Kennedy sends Averill Harriman to Moscow for talks.

At his news conference the president voices concern at what would happen if the Reds take over.

"It's important as a sovereign power people desire to be independent. And it's also important because it borders the Mekong River and quite obviously if Laos fell under Communist hands, it would increase the danger along the northern frontiers of Thailand. It would put additional pressure on Cambodia and would put additional pressure on Malaya. So I do accept the view that there is an interrelationship in these countries and that's one of the reasons why we're concerned with maintaining the Geneva Accords as a method of maintaining stability in Southeast Asia. It may be one of the reasons why others do not share that interest."

WHAT A YEAR IT WAS!

ASIA ────── 1963

VIETNAM

◆ 30 reported dead as Viet Cong down five U.S. helicopters in Mekong Delta.

◆ The U.S. advises South Vietnam's **PRESIDENT NGO DINH**.

◆ U.S. predicts all U.S. forces in Vietnam could be withdrawn by 1965.

◆ New regime in Saigon recognized by the U.S.

◆ The "suicides" of South Vietnam's **PRESIDENT NGO DINH DIEM** and his brother **NGO DINH NHU** are reported following the toppling of their government by a military coup.

KOREA

◆ Following intense pressure from the people of South Korea and the U.S. government, **GENERAL PARK CHUNG HEE** holds elections and is elected to a four-year term as president after eliminating most of his opponents.

Mongolia

Japan

Korea

China

Tibet

Nepal

India

Burma

Laos

Thailand

Vietnam

Cambodia

Ceylon

Philippines

CHINA

◆ U.N. votes to bar Communist China.

◆ China extends invitation to **PREMIER NIKITA KHRUSHCHEV** to visit Peking.

INDIA

◆ India refuses to recognize China-Pakistan border pact.

1963 DEAN RUSK

Chairman Khrushchev's villa on the Black Sea is the scene of informal meetings between the Soviet boss and Secretary of State Dean Rusk.

These high-level meetings follow on the heels of an East-West atom test ban.

Mr. Khrushchev (*left*) and Mr. Rusk (*right*) touch on many things in a relaxed atmosphere and finally the U.S., Britain and the U.S.S.R. sign a Partial Test Ban Treaty, banning nuclear tests in the atmosphere, ocean and space where radioactive debris could extend beyond territorial limits.

The meeting adjourns to a recreation room where Mr. Khrushchev takes on Mr. Rusk at a game of badminton.

Decked out in his Ukrainian blouse, the Russian leader defeats the American. But that's the life of a diplomat. A rare and informal portrait of behind-the-scenes diplomacy.

WHAT A YEAR IT WAS!

VISITS RUSSIA AND GERMANY ON ATOM BOMB TREATY

On his way home from Moscow, Mr. Rusk arrives in Bonn to discuss the atom test ban treaty with Chancellor Adenauer.

West German leaders are reluctant to sign the treaty, fearing that it might lead to recognition of East Germany as a legal government. Mr. Rusk seeks to reassure the West German government.

After a seven-hour meeting, an agreement is reached. West Germany will sign the pact, relying on the U.S. pledge that Bonn will be consulted on future negotiations with Moscow.

WHAT A YEAR IT WAS!

A crowd assembles outside the United Nations to see President Kennedy.

*P*resident Kennedy arrives with Ambassador Adlai Stevenson *(left)* and is welcomed by Secretary-General U Thant *(center)* and American delegate Dr. Ralph Bunche *(right)*.

WHAT A YEAR IT WAS!

KENNEDY ── 1963

Addresses The United Nations 18th General Assembly on a Joint Venture with the Soviets on Space Travel

*P*resident Kennedy is the first of many heads of state who are scheduled to address the Assembly.

*M*r. Kennedy hails the pause in the Cold War while taking note of Cuba and Berlin. Then he makes a startling proposal.

"Finally, in a field where the United States and the Soviet Union have a special capacity, in the field of space, there is room for new cooperation for further joint efforts in the regulation and exploration of space. I include among these possibilities a joint expedition to the moon. Space offers no problems of sovereignty. By resolution of this Assembly, the members of the United Nations have foresworn any claim to the territorial rights in outer space or on celestial bodies and declare that international law and the United Nations charter will apply. Why therefore should man's first flight to the moon be a matter of national competition? Why should the United States and the Soviet Union in preparing for such expeditions become involved in immense duplications of research, construction and expenditure?"

WHAT A YEAR IT WAS!

NIKITA KHRUSHCHEV VISITS THE BERLIN WALL.

MOSCOW OFFERS TO ALLOW ON-SITE INSPECTIONS OF NUCLEAR TESTING.

U.S.S.R. and France sign trade agreement.

TENSIONS BETWEEN THE SOVIET UNION AND THE UNITED STATES MOUNT OVER THE SOVIET MILITARY PRESENCE IN CUBA, WITH MOSCOW THREATENING WAR IF U.S. ATTACKS CUBA.

THE TENTH ANNIVERSARY OF STALIN'S DEATH IS IGNORED IN RUSSIA.

Despite pleas from Soviet Premier Nikita Khrushchev, top Communist Julian Grimau Garcia is executed in Madrid.

U.S. ENVOY REFUSES TO ATTEND MAY DAY CEREMONIES IN MOSCOW BECAUSE OF THE PRESENCE OF CASTRO.

CHARGING THE U.N. WITH PRO-WEST BIAS, THE SOVIET UNION WITHHOLDS PAYMENT OF ITS DUES.

RUSSIA + CHINA =

■ After two weeks of secret meetings in Moscow, Communist China and Soviet Russia fail to resolve their ideological differences.

■ Soviets offer India weapons to block China.

■ Soviet Union accuses China of over 5,000 border violations.

WHAT A YEAR IT WAS!

EUROPE

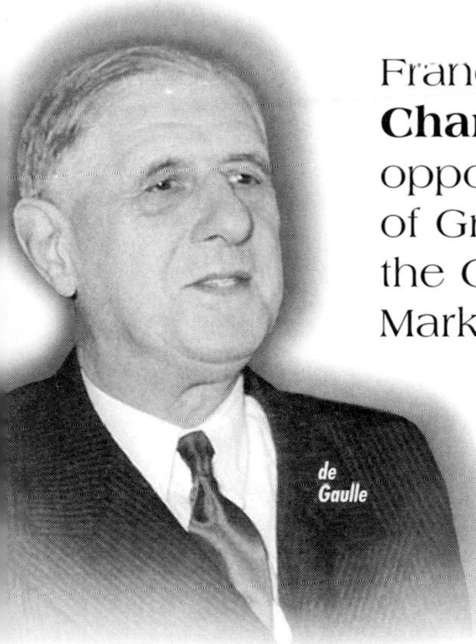

France's President **Charles de Gaulle** opposes the admission of Great Britain to the Common Market.

HAROLD WILSON elected by the British Labour Party as foreign affairs spokesman.

HAROLD MACMILLAN resigns as British prime minister and is succeeded by the 14th earl of Home – SIR ALEC DOUGLAS-HOME.

Five people receive death sentences in a plot to kill **President de Gaulle**.

de Gaulle

Norway
Sweden
Finlan
United Kingdom
Denmark
Holland
Belgium
Luxembourg
Poland
Germany
Czechoslovakia
France
Switzerland
Austria
Hungary
Portugal
Italy
Yugoslavia
Spain
Albania
Greece

U.S. announces plans to sell plutonium to France.

WILLY BRANDT reelected mayor of West Berlin.

MARSHAL TITO
to rule for life under the new Yugoslavian constitution.

Tito

■ **France announces its withdrawal from the NATO fleet in the North Atlantic.**

■ **A U.S. convoy held for 41 hours in East Germany is released following protests from the West.**

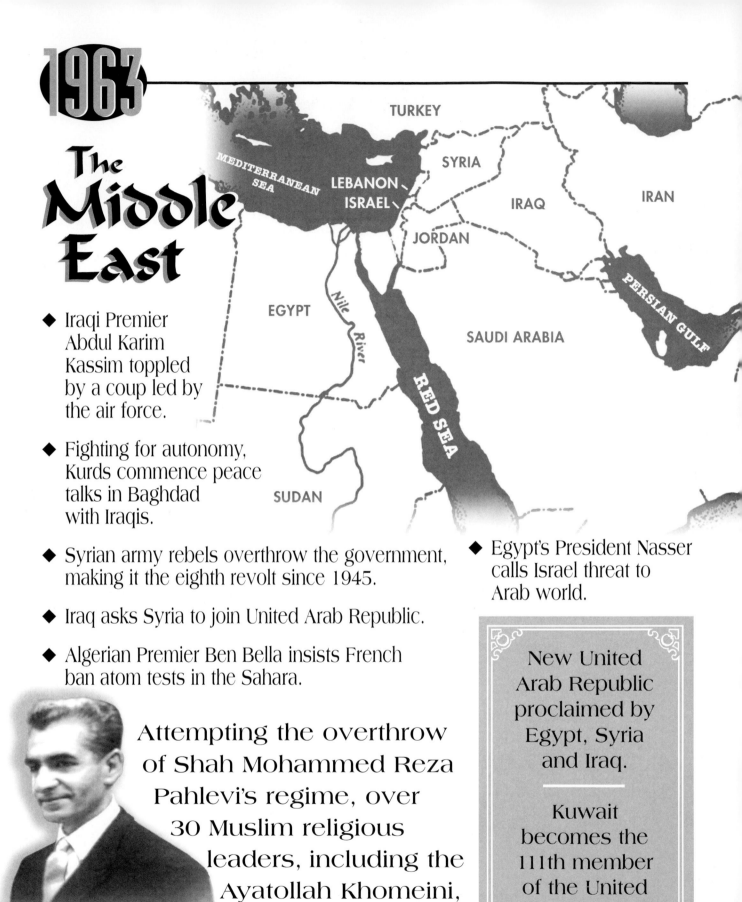

1963

The Middle East

◆ Iraqi Premier Abdul Karim Kassim toppled by a coup led by the air force.

◆ Fighting for autonomy, Kurds commence peace talks in Baghdad with Iraqis.

◆ Syrian army rebels overthrow the government, making it the eighth revolt since 1945.

◆ Iraq asks Syria to join United Arab Republic.

◆ Algerian Premier Ben Bella insists French ban atom tests in the Sahara.

◆ Egypt's President Nasser calls Israel threat to Arab world.

Attempting the overthrow of Shah Mohammed Reza Pahlevi's regime, over 30 Muslim religious leaders, including the Ayatollah Khomeini, are arrested in Iran.

Shah Mohammed Reza Pahlevi
(The Shah of Iran)

New United Arab Republic proclaimed by Egypt, Syria and Iraq.

———

Kuwait becomes the 111th member of the United Nations.

Public phones are found in the likeliest places!

Public phones are handy everywhere. We put them on streets and highways, corners and crossings, in parks, stores, stations, lobbies, terminals—wherever they're needed. They can save time, help you make dates, chat with friends, find directions, get aid in a hurry. So look for them, and use them as you use your phones at home.

Bell Telephone System

19

1963

CANADA

Conservative government led by Canada's Premier Diefenbaker ousted by coalition.

Canada's Premier Lester Pearson agrees to accept U.S. warheads.

UNITED STATES

The Americans and Soviets approve a diplomatic hot line between Washington and Moscow designed to reduce the risk of accidental war.

U.S. ousts Soviet diplomat Gennadi Sevastyanov for attempting to recruit a CIA agent.

New York Governor Nelson A. Rockefeller issues a statement condemning "the radical right" wing of the Republican Party, the John Birch Society and "others of the radical right lunatic fringe," who he said are as dangerous to America as "the radical left."

Governor Rockefeller announces his candidacy for the Republican nomination for president.

Fidel Castro

100 U.S. citizens arrive in Miami from Cuba.

U.S. reports all Soviet offensive arms have been removed from Cuba.

Cuba receives warning from U.S. after MiGs fire rockets near American shrimp boat.

Cuban government expropriates U.S. Embassy and grounds in Havana.

Cuba's Fidel Castro calls President Kennedy "the Batista of his time."

Cuba accuses the U.S. of raiding one of its air force bases.

LATIN AMERICA

An American freighter is seized by Venezuelan Communists who seek asylum in Brazil.

GUATEMALAN PRESIDENT MIGUEL FUENTES is overthrown by military junta.

ARGENTINA cancels all foreign oil contracts.

WHAT A YEAR IT WAS!

Africa

TSHOMBE

U.N. rejects Katanga President Moise Tshombe's request for truce talks.

* Congo's central government takes over Katanga on an interim basis.

* President Tshombe placed under house arrest by the U.N.

Moise Tshombe

* President Tshombe agrees to reunite the province with the rest of the Congo provided he and his followers are granted amnesty.

Leaders of 30 independent African states adopt a charter creating an Organization of African Unity.

U.S. announces to the United Nations that it will halt sale of weapons to South Africa.

KENYA

JOMO KENYATTA ELECTED FIRST PRIME MINISTER OF KENYA.

CONGO throws out Soviet aides and severs ties to **MOSCOW**.

After 73 years of British rule, Zanzibar regains independence.

Nnamdi Azikiwe becomes first president of the new republic of Nigeria.

PASSINGS

Estes Kefauver (60)

Herbert Henry Lehman (85)

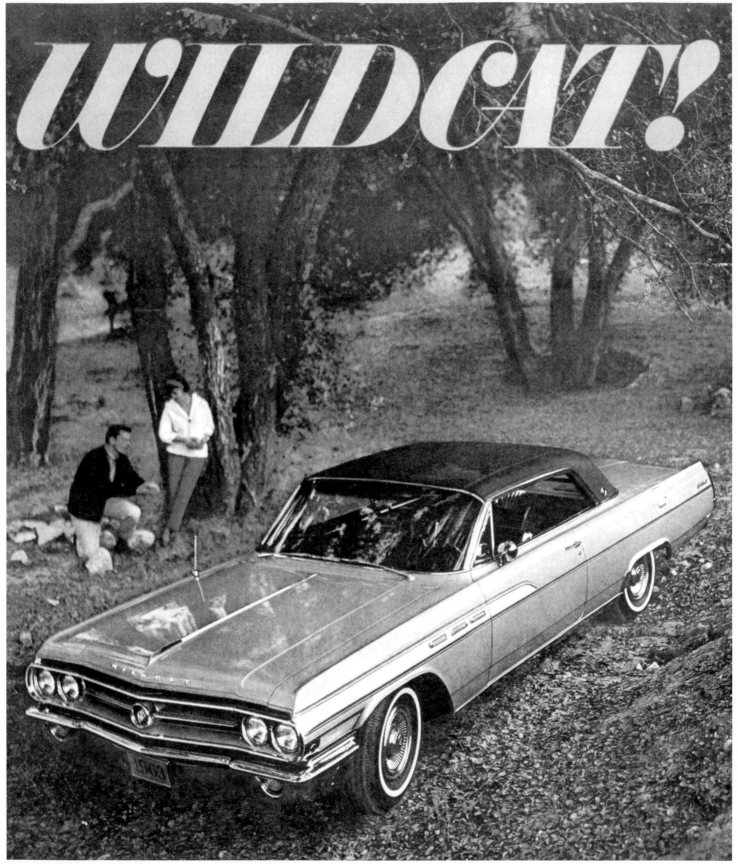

Anatomy of a *WILDCAT!* External characteristics . . . sleek, sure-footed, muscular—325-hp strong. Three distinct types—convertible, 2-dr. sport coupe, 4-dr. hardtop. Internal structure . . . V-8, 401 cu. in. Wildcat engine. 10.25:1 compression ratio. 4-bbl. downdraft carburetor. Automatic Turbine Drive transmission. 12" brakes—finned aluminum up front. Temperament . . . terribly impatient in captivity. Thrives best out on the wide open road (tracks straight as an arrow, corners like a cat). Habitat . . . your Buick dealer's.

Buick Motor Division also presents: Buick Special/Skylark/LeSabre/Electra 225/Riviera

22

WILDCAT BY BUICK!

PEOPLE — 1963

PRESIDENT KENNEDY PRESENTS BOB HOPE WITH A GOLD MEDAL
Honoring Him for Bringing Laughter to G.I.s in the Remotest Corners of the Globe.

"It's been one of the rarest honors given to an American and it's a great pleasure for me on behalf of the Congress to present this to you. It's a splendid picture of you. I hope everyone has a chance to look at it."

"Thank you very much, Mr. President. That's very nice. I suggested to Senator Symington I should have had a nose job, but he said there would've been less gold. But I actually don't like to tell jokes about a thing like this because it's one of the nicest things that's ever happened to me and I feel very humble. Although I think I have the strength of character to fight it."

"I also want to say that I played in the South Pacific while the president was there, and he was a very gay, carefree young man at that time. Of course, all he had to worry about at that time was the enemy."

GENERAL
DOUGLAS MACARTHUR
HONORED

New Accolades For An Old Soldier

Celebrating his 83rd birthday in New York, General Douglas MacArthur is honored with the establishment of the MacArthur Chair in History at Columbia University.

Mrs. MacArthur (*left*) looks on as Governor Rockefeller (*right*) and other distinguished guests extol the general as "one who made living history."

The man who put "I shall return" into the language is called "a legend in his own time."

WHAT A YEAR IT WAS!

John F. Kennedy creates the blue, white
and gold Presidential Medal of Freedom, the nation's
highest civilian honor, to be awarded annually to persons
"who contribute significantly to the quality of American life."

Ralph Bunche

Marian Anderson

FIRST RECIPIENTS
OF THE PRESIDENTIAL
MEDAL OF FREEDOM

(a sampling)

Felix Frankfurter

MARIAN ANDERSON
SINGER

RALPH BUNCHE
U.N. DIPLOMAT

ELLSWORTH BUNKER
INDUSTRIALIST

PABLO CASALS
CELLIST/CONDUCTOR

JAMES B. CONANT
SCIENTIST

JOHN F. ENDERS
NOBEL PRIZE FOR MEDICINE

FELIX FRANKFURTER
SUPREME COURT JUSTICE (FORMER)

HERBERT LEHMAN
U.S. SENATOR (FORMER)

GEORGE MEANY
LABOR LEADER

RUDOLF SERKIN
CONCERT PIANIST

PRESIDENT KENNEDY makes **SIR WINSTON CHURCHILL** an honorary U.S. citizen.

A SAD DAY FOR THE KENNEDYS

Jacqueline Kennedy gives birth to Patrick Bouvier Kennedy, who dies two days later of a lung disease common in premature infants. After a miscarriage in 1955 and a stillbirth in 1956, this is the third loss for the Kennedys.

FATHER OF THE YEAR
(National Father's Day Committee)
John F. Kennedy, Jr.

WHAT A YEAR IT WAS!

PRESIDENT
ASSASSINATED

President Kennedy, with his wife, Jacqueline, arrives in Dallas around noon following a tumultuous reception in Fort Worth where he addressed a crowd in a parking lot near his hotel, saying:

> *"Mrs. Kennedy is organizing herself. It takes longer. Of course, she looks better than we do when she does it."*

Later at a breakfast meeting, the president notes his wife's presence by saying:

> *"Two years ago, I introduced myself in Paris by saying that I was the man who had accompanied Mrs. Kennedy to Paris. I am getting somewhat the same sensation as I travel around Texas. Nobody wonders what Lyndon and I wear."*

Thousands of people are waiting to greet him in downtown Dallas. Death is less than one short hour away.

At 1:25 p.m. the motorcade moves into the downtown area. Death is six minutes away.

The motorcade winds its way along a 10-mile route. Mrs. Kennedy, who seldom accompanies her husband on political outings, appears to be enjoying herself.

In a warehouse a sniper with a rifle poised waits.

The cheers of the crowd almost muffle the three shots. The assassin's aim is deadly and the area is aswarm with police, rangers and Secret Service men.

WHAT A YEAR IT WAS!

KENNEDY
IN DALLAS

The murderer slips through the net, but within the hour, Patrolman J.D. Tippit sights the suspect, who pulls out a revolver and shoots the officer. At 2:15 p.m., police capture Oswald in a movie theater a few blocks away.

The alleged assassin is a 24-year-old former marine and pro-Castro Texan, Lee Harvey Oswald, who once sought Soviet citizenship and has been active in the Fair Play for Cuba Committee. He is believed to have fired at least three shots from a rifle as he stood in the Texas School Book Depository where he was employed. Oswald is charged with murder.

DALLAS POLICE 54018 11 23 63

With Mrs. Kennedy cradling her husband's body, the president, with a gaping, massive wound to his head, is rushed to a nearby hospital where his life lingers.

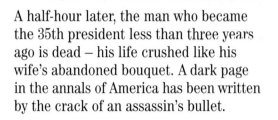

A half-hour later, the man who became the 35th president less than three years ago is dead – his life crushed like his wife's abandoned bouquet. A dark page in the annals of America has been written by the crack of an assassin's bullet.

Cheering crowds who line the streets are stunned.

KEEP RIGHT

WHAT A YEAR IT WAS!

A shocked nation weeps. Across the country and around the world disbelief is the first reaction. Then, a great outpouring of grief, shock and revulsion.

A proud banner is lowered.

The empty White House is a symbol of this infamous mockery of the American ideals of peace and freedom.

Peoples of all faiths unite in prayer for the first Catholic to become president.

WHAT A YEAR IT WAS!

ASSASSINATED IN DALLAS

The United Nations General Assembly joins in a minute of silent tribute to the man who fought so hard and valiantly for the ideals of this international body.

Reporters gather on the runway at Love Field.

DEMOCRACY FINDS ITS STRENGTH in the continuity of the presidency and just 99 minutes after Kennedy's death, Lyndon B. Johnson is sworn in as the 36th president of the United States on Air Force One by Judge Sarah T. Hughes. With a sorrowful face and still wearing the raspberry-colored suit, Mrs. Kennedy stands bravely by the new president's side.

President Johnson speaks:

"This is a sad time for all people. We have suffered a loss that cannot be weighed. For me, it is a deep personal tragedy. I know that the world shares the sorrow that Mrs. Kennedy and her family bear. I will do my best. That is all I can do. I ask for your help and God's."

WHAT A YEAR IT WAS!

PRESIDENT KENNEDY
REMEMBERED

And so the nation and the world mourn the loss of a young president who led his country boldly through the treacherous shoals of Cold War crises.

His firm commitments to support the cause of democracy throughout the world won him acclaim almost unprecedented in the history of the presidency. He faced up to Communist threats with such firm shows of force that Khrushchev backed down in Cuba and softened the hard Red line on Berlin.

He brought to the White House the vigor of youth and a family that captivated the hearts of all as depicted in this last group picture of his family – John and Jacqueline, John-John and Caroline.

In the speech that he did not live to deliver, President Kennedy was going to attack right-wing conservatives, saying that:

"...voices are being heard in the land, voices preaching doctrines wholly unrelated to reality, wholly unsuited to the sixties, doctrines which apparently assume that words will suffice without weapons, that vituperation is as good as victory and that peace is a sign of weakness."

President Kennedy and Mayor Willy Brandt in Berlin where Kennedy, addressing a crowd of over 150,000, makes his "*ich bin ein Berliner*" speech. Almost a quarter of Berlin's 2.5 million citizens turn out to greet President Kennedy during his four-day trip to West Germany.

Immortalizing President John F. Kennedy At Home And Abroad

Rue Clemenceau in **BEIRUT** is renamed *Kennedy Street*.

WEST BERLIN's city hall square is dedicated as *John F. Kennedy Platz* and Bonn's Rhine bridge is renamed the *Kennedy Brücke*.

President Johnson asks Congress to approve the minting of a *50¢ coin* bearing a portrait of the late President Kennedy.

HARVARD President Nathan M. Pusey announces that articles of incorporation have been filed for the *John F. Kennedy Memorial Library* to be erected on a 2-acre site donated by the university.

A bill is introduced in Congress to name the proposed national cultural center the *John Fitzgerald Kennedy Memorial Center*.

The annual peace award of the **SYNAGOGUE COUNCIL OF AMERICA** is renamed the *John Fitzgerald Kennedy Peace Award*.

The new Ohio River bridge is dedicated as the *John Fitzgerald Kennedy Memorial Bridge*.

The **N.Y. CITY** Council votes to rename the N.Y. International Airport (Idlewild) the *John F. Kennedy International Airport*.

President Johnson announces the renaming of Cape Canaveral to *Cape Kennedy* and its space installations would be called the *John F. Kennedy Space Center*.

PRESIDENT KENNEDY'S WILL directs that the bulk of his estate be divided into two equal shares – one of which is to be held in trust for his wife, Jacqueline, and the other held in trust for his two children, Caroline, 6, and John Jr., 3, with Mrs. Kennedy designated executor of the estate and a trustee of the trusts.

JACQUELINE KENNEDY PURCHASES a 169-year-old, three-story, 14-room brick home in the Georgetown section of Washington.

THE U.S. SENATE passes a bill granting Jacqueline Kennedy Secret Service protection, a temporary secretarial staff, office space and free mailing privileges for life, in addition to her widow's pension of $10,000 a year for life or until she remarries.

President Kennedy's two dead children – an unnamed girl and Patrick Bouvier Kennedy – are reburied next to the late president at Arlington National Cemetery.

1963

PRESIDENT JOHNSON
ASSUMES BURDEN OF OFFICE

The United States of America and the world listen as President Lyndon B. Johnson addresses a joint session of Congress. The occasion is solemn, his tone somber.

"I am here today to say I need your help. I cannot bear this burden alone. I need the help of all Americans in all America. John Kennedy's death commands what his life conveyed - that America must move forward."

PRESIDENT JOHNSON, ALONG WITH APPROXIMATELY 14,000 PEOPLE, ATTENDS A CANDLELIGHT SERVICE AT THE LINCOLN MEMORIAL ENDING THE 30-DAY PERIOD OF NATIONAL MOURNING.

An article in the WASHINGTON POST by **NATE HAZELTINE REPORTS** that President Kennedy was killed by the second of the two assassination bullets and could have survived the first bullet, which was found deep in the shoulder.

THE FBI CONCLUDES that Lee Harvey Oswald acted alone in the assassination of President John F. Kennedy.

THE ZAPRUDER FILM, an amateur film of the Kennedy assassination, shows Texas governor John Connally being shot 1.8 seconds after the president and leads to controversy over whether the same bullet hit both men and the possibility of a conspiracy.

President Johnson names Chief Justice Earl Warren to head a commission of inquiry into the Kennedy assassination.

Dallas nightclub owner Jack Ruby shoots and kills Lee Harvey Oswald, accused killer of President Kennedy, in the basement of a Dallas jail as millions witness the murder on television. His attorney later describes Ruby as a very emotional man who killed out of sympathy for Jackie Kennedy.

the private world of Jerry Lewis

How to make a spacious 34-room house a warm, inviting home has been admirably achieved by Jerry's wife, Patti. In this large living room, vividly colored sofas, low tables and dramatic lamps are grouped into invitingly intimate conversation corners, preserving a look of uncluttered simplicity. For her living room carpeting she chose a custom shag, off-white wool. In other rooms, Patti's good taste has its practical side, with easy-to-clean Royalweve carpeting of continuous-filament Nylon. It thrives on punishment, come what may from five junior editions of Jerry. Have you been wishing for beautiful carpeting, even though you have a houseful of youngsters? Take Jerry and Patti's suggestion and see your Royalweve dealer. He has the answers for you...beginning at only $6.95 a yard! **ROYALWEVE CARPETS**

CALIFORNIA CREATED FOR
EVERY FOOT OF AMERICA
HAND CARPET MILLS
LOS ANGELES 58 CALIF.

Watch for JERRY LEWIS' forthcoming production, *"The NUTTY professor"*

33

1963

Princess Grace AND *Prince Rainier* VISIT NEW YORK

Prince Rainier III of Monaco arrives in New York with his daughter, Caroline, for a six-week visit in the U.S. His princess, the former Grace Kelly, is arriving on a later flight with their son, Prince Albert, heir to the throne. Prince Rainier and the former movie star will celebrate their seventh wedding anniversary during their visit.

Four hours later Princess Grace arrives with little Prince Albert. The family is leaving immediately for Philadelphia, Grace's old hometown, where they will open a travel exhibit and dedicate a theater at Raven Hill Academy in memory of her father. Though a titled princess, Her Highness says she remains a Philadelphia girl at heart.

EMPERORS...PRINCES...PRINCESSES

THERE'S SOMETHING FISHY HERE

Following in the footsteps of his father, Emperor Hirohito, Japan's most famous Sunday marine microbiologist, **CROWN PRINCE AKIHITO**, completes a treatise on the shoulder blades of the goby fish and announces at his 30th birthday press conference a tonic devised to restore the appetite of his wife, Princess Michiko, still ill after a March abortion.

14-year-old **PRINCE CHARLES** takes his first ski lesson in Schuls, Switzerland.

19-year-old Sweden's **PRINCESS CHRISTINA** is entering Radcliffe College, Harvard's "sister school."

WHAT A YEAR IT WAS!

QUEEN ELIZABETH II 1963
VISITS NEW ZEALAND

Her majesty's yacht **Britannia** sails into the Bay of Plenty as Queen Elizabeth begins her visit to New Zealand.

The Queen and Prince Philip receive a warm welcome.

Led by their chiefs, 10,000 Maoris gather to meet their queen.

These Polynesian natives first landed in New Zealand six centuries ago and brought with them the high culture of their islands.

As the chants fade away 10,000 miles from the seat of the British throne, the Queen finds warmth that transcends mere loyalty to the Crown. The sun never sets on the people who   love her.

Part of their tradition is a ceremonial war dance in honor of their leader from across the seas.

1963

Most Admired Americans
Gallup Poll

MEN:		WOMEN:
President Lyndon Johnson	**1**	Mrs. Jacqueline Kennedy
Dwight D. Eisenhower **(FORMER PRESIDENT)**	**2**	Mrs. Lyndon Johnson
Sir Winston Churchill	**3**	Queen Elizabeth II
Albert Schweitzer	**4**	Senator Margaret Chase Smith
Robert F. Kennedy	**5**	Mrs. Mamie Eisenhower
Rev. Billy Graham	**6**	Mrs. Clare Boothe Luce
Adlai E. Stevenson	**7**	Helen Keller
Pope Paul VI	**8**	Princess Grace of Monaco
Charles de Gaulle	**9**	Mrs. Ngo Dinh Nhu
Richard M. Nixon	**10**	Marian Anderson

Adlai Stevenson

Mamie Eisenhower

Martin Luther King, Jr.

TIME

MAN OF THE YEAR

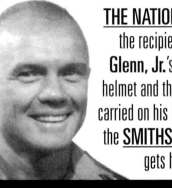

THE NATIONAL AIR MUSEUM is the recipient of astronaut **John H. Glenn, Jr.**'s silver space suit, boots, helmet and the small American flag he carried on his historic triple orbit while the **SMITHSONIAN INSTITUTION** gets his **Freedom 7** capsule.

Happy Birthday, Bubala
400 students from the Hebrew University parade in front of Martin Buber's home in Jerusalem in honor of his 85th birthday.

NO "DUCKING" THIS AWARD
WALT DISNEY named winner of the 14th annual $5,000 George Washington Award by the Freedoms Foundation in Valley Forge, Pa.

WHAT A YEAR IT WAS!

Awards & Recognitions

At a posh luncheon in New York, Columbia College announces a $500,000 endowment for a General Douglas MacArthur Chair in History.

Welcome, Pilgrims

Former President Dwight D. Eisenhower receives the gold medal from the Pilgrims of the United States for "great contributions to the cause of Anglo-American unity."

I SAY, IS THAT A WOMAN I SEE LURKING IN THE DOORWAY?

Helen Hayes becomes the first woman ever invited inside the Bohemian Club's private dining room.

The Democratic representative from Georgia, George Carl Vinson, sets a record by serving in the House longer than any person in history – 48 years, 8 months, 13 days.

JUST DON'T REACH FOR THE AJAX

Joan Crawford, veteran screen star and widow of Pepsi-Cola Chairman Alfred M. Steele, receives an award from the Philadelphia Club of Advertising Women.

WHAT A YEAR IT WAS!

PERSONALITIES

Getting ready for his bout with heavyweight Doug Jones at Madison Square Garden, 20-year-old **CASSIUS MARCELLUS CLAY** does a little sparring with poetry at Greenwich Village's Bitter End where he recites "Ode to a Champion: Cassius Marcellus Clay."

What's A Poor Rich Guy To Do?

Appearing on a television program in England, billionaire J. Paul Getty confesses that money is everything and that he wishes he "had a better personality so he could entertain better." Party mavin Elsa Maxwell agrees with him, calling him "the dullest man that ever lived and socially impossible."

They Got No Kick Out Of Rudy

Following an opening-night party with prima ballerina Dame Margot Fonteyn, defected Soviet dancer Rudolf Nureyev is busted in Toronto for pirouetting along the white center line of Yonge Street and some high kicks.

So There !!

Sophia Loren is declared unfit to be godmother to the granddaughter of Benito Mussolini as long as Italian and church law block Carlo Ponti's divorce from his wife and marriage to Sophia. Despite this ruling, she declares, "I am the child's godmother and proud of it."

If You Can't Stand The Heat, Leave The House

Betty Friedan writes the explosive THE FEMININE MYSTIQUE, which attacks the myth of the happy homemaker.

1963
Coupling

Carol Burnett **&** Joseph Hamilton

Nelson Rockefeller **&** Margaretta "Happy" Murphy

Paul Anka **&** Anne DeZogheb

Betty White **&** Allen Ludden

Cher **&** Sonny Bono

Anita Ekberg **&** Rik Van Nutter

Edith Mack Hirsch **&** Desi Arnaz

Rick Nelson **&** Kristin Harmon

Joan Collins **&** Anthony Newley

Dinah Shore **&** Maurice Fabian Smith

Robert Shaw **&** Mary Ure

Barbra Streisand **&** Elliott Gould

Gloria Vanderbilt **&** Wyatt Cooper

Robert Wagner **&** Marion Marshall

Brenda Lee **&** Charles Ronald Shacklett

Hedy Lamarr **&** Lewis Boies, Jr.

Suzy Parker **&** Bradford Dillman

Judy Carne **&** Burt Reynolds

John Lennon **&** Cynthia Powell

Tony Curtis **&** Christine Kaufmann

Johnny Weissmuller **&** Maria Bauman

Actress Joan Fontaine squelches rumors that she is going to marry cartoonist Charles Adams.

WHAT A YEAR IT WAS!

Uncoupling

Richard Burton **&** Sybil Burton

Linda Darnell **&** Merle Robertson

Norman Mailer **&** Lady Jeanne Campbell

Anthony Newley **&** Ann Lynn

Penny Marshall **&** Michael Henry

Ernest Borgnine **&** Katy Jurado

Peter Sellers **&** Anne Howe Sellers

IS EVERYBODY "HAPPY"?

Following the divorce from his wife of 31 years and marriage to divorcée Mrs. Margaretta Fitler Murphy, Nelson Rockefeller's chances to be the Republican Party's presidential candidate are diminished because of a "badly tarnished image."

•

According to a Gallup Poll, Nelson Rockefeller has fallen in popularity following his divorce and remarriage to a divorcée.

Robert Goulet **&** Louise Longmore Goulet

Exciting new blend of beauty and action... in the low-price field!

Championship style...

and performance to back it up!

Playgoers call it poise, sportsmen call it class! By any name, Cutlass has it to spare . . . the jaunty self-confidence that says, "Look me over, I'm a winner!" It packs an ultra high-compression V-8 engine that generates up to 195 horsepower! Parks in the tightest places—turns full circle in a mere 37 feet! And cradles you in bucket-seat comfort through it all! Try Oldsmobile's lowest-priced sports car—an F-85 Cutlass—today!

There's "SOMETHING EXTRA" about owning an OLDSMOBILE!

F-85
Cutlass
by
OLDSMOBILE
Oldsmobile Division • General Motors Corporation

40

ILLS of the RICH & FAMOUS

76-year-old **T. S. ELIOT** is suffering from a bronchial attack precipitated by London's recent heavy smog.

EDWARD R. MURROW, U.S. Information Agency Director, undergoes surgery for the removal of a lung due to cancer.

MAMIE EISENHOWER has come down with a touch of flu in Palm Desert, California.

Former president **HARRY S. TRUMAN** is recovering after a hernia operation.

Actor **VAN JOHNSON** undergoes surgery for skin cancer.

Singer **JUDY GARLAND** comes down with the flu in London.

BETTE DAVIS, 54, is battling the flu and is confined to her room at Manhattan's Plaza Hotel.

Bandleader **TED WEEMS**, 62, is on the critical list after an emergency tracheotomy at Hillcrest Medical Center in Tulsa.

Bette Davis

WHAT A YEAR IT WAS!

DAME JUDITH ANDERSON's performances in *Medea* and *Macbeth* are interrupted when she comes down with a case of the flu in Asheville, North Carolina.

30-year-old **ELIZABETH TAYLOR** dislocates cartilage in her left knee while on the set of her new film, *The V.I.P.s.*

MARIA CALLAS, 39, is recovering in her Milan apartment following surgery to correct a hernia.

CARROLL BAKER is down with mononucleosis in London.

44-year-old **BILLY GRAHAM** is hospitalized in Honolulu with an intestinal infection.

Crooner **BING CROSBY** is in a Santa Monica hospital for removal of kidney stones.

Irish playwright **BRENDAN BEHAN** is in the hospital for the fourth time in 18 months.

Oscar nominee **BURT LANCASTER** is down with infectious hepatitis.

Former first lady **MAMIE EISENHOWER** is resting nicely in Walter Reed General Hospital after the removal of a benign tumor from her neck.

88-year-old former president **HERBERT HOOVER** is quite ill due to bleeding from his gastrointestinal tract.

Harry S. Truman

Maria Callas

Judy Garland

Bing Crosby

Crimes & Misde

NO LAUGHING MATTER

Comedian Lenny Bruce is declared a drug addict and ordered confined to a California rehabilitation center by a Los Angeles Superior Court judge.

HEY, YOU SQUEALIN' ON ME?

With a $100,000 "bounty" on his head, convicted killer Joseph M. Valachi testifies before the Senate Investigations Committee, naming "King of the Rackets" Vito Genovese as the "boss of bosses" of the underworld's "Cosa Nostra" as well as naming the crime families and their 12 U.S. centers.

NEW MAILING ADDRESS

38-year-old Texan **Billie Sol Estes** is sentenced to 15 years in prison for mail fraud and conspiracy, having swindled a dozen major finance companies of $24 million worth of mortgage deals.

JIMMY HOFFA'S ATTORNEY is disbarred for attempted jury tampering in Nashville during the Teamster president's conspiracy trial last year. Four more people are indicted on the same charge, bringing the total number of indictments to 10.

The High Price Of Sex

Following the exposure of his affair with 21-year-old prostitute **CHRISTINE KEELER**, illustrious politician British Secretary of War **JOHN PROFUMO** is forced to resign.

Osteopath Dr. Stephen Ward, doctor in the John Profumo case, takes an overdose of drugs, goes into a coma and dies following being found guilty of running a prostitution ring.

EXTRA

Attorney General **Robert Kennedy** indicts 81 Teamster officials.

WHAT A YEAR IT WAS!

neanors

SINGING A HAPPY TUNE

Frank Sinatra, Jr. is home safe in his parents' homes after being kidnapped from a Lake Tahoe casino for a $240,000 ransom.

PAUL McCARTNEY is fined 31 pounds and given a one-year suspended license for speeding.

Professor **TIMOTHY LEARY** is dismissed from Harvard over LSD controversy.

A PURRRRTY BIG SCORE

A cat burglar makes off with $193,000 in jewelry from the Manhasset, Long Island estate of Mr. & Mrs. William S. Paley, which includes a 12-carat emerald and diamond ring valued at $77,000 and a $50,000 diamond necklace containing 78 stones.

1963

SEEING RED

Presumed to be in hiding behind the Iron Curtain, newspaper correspondent **Kim Philby** is named a Soviet spy by the British government, which says he's been working for the Soviets since 1946.

HE AIN'T NO STINKIN' SPY

John Steinbeck and Edward Albee denounce the arrest in Moscow of Yale professor Frederick Barghoorn on spy charges.

After a five-year self-imposed exile to escape the "Red" inquisition, singer **Paul Robeson** returns to the U.S.

International publicity agent and society columnist **Igor Cassini** is indicted by a Washington federal grand jury for failing to register as an agent of the Dominican Republic's former Trujillo regime.

One For The Hall Of Shame

Birmingham Police Chief Bull Connor uses police dogs, fire hoses and cattle prods on Martin Luther King, Jr. and the marching schoolchildren and adults in Birmingham.

Black student James Meredith graduates from the University of Mississippi.

Muslim national leader Elijah Muhammad, scheduled to be the main speaker at the Black Muslim convention in Chicago, is too ill to attend and is replaced by Malcolm X.

1963

Birthdays and Celebrations

CATHERINE DENEUVE gives birth to Roger Vadim's son – Christian Vadim.

BOBBY and **ETHEL KENNEDY** are expecting their eighth child.

How Sweet It Is
BOB HOPE celebrates his 60th birthday with a family party at home including a cake with three candy golf balls.

International party animal **ELSA MAXWELL** turns 80 and receives roses from Princess Grace and over 800 telegrams.

Retirements

JOHN L. LEWIS retires as president of the United Mine Workers of America.

ONE DRINK TOO MANY
President of Ecuador Carlos Arosemena is "retired" by a military coup for hitting the bottle too often.

Having served his country since 1900, guiding Britain through the critical years of World War II, **SIR WINSTON CHURCHILL** announces his retirement.

Citing personal needs, **DAVID BEN-GURION** resigns as Israeli premier, relinquishes his post as defense minister and gives up his seat in the Knesset.

West German **CHANCELLOR KONRAD ADENAUER** retires after 14 years as head of the government and is replaced by Ludwig Erhard.

David Ben-Gurion

"Tricky Dick" GOES BACK TO HIS OLD PROFESSION
Richard M. Nixon, who appears to have given up politics, moves to New York and becomes a partner in a prestigious law firm.

Richard Nixon

...AND NOW FOR A DIFFERENT KIND OF SONG AND DANCE
Song-and-dance man **George Murphy** announces that he is seeking the Republican nomination for U.S. Senator.

POPE JOHN XXIII issues a plea for world political unity in his 8th encyclical letter, *Pacem in Terris*.

The Mantle Is Passed On

Following the death of 81-year-old Pope John XXIII from complications of stomach cancer, the archbishop of Milan, 65-year-old Giovanni Battista Cardinal Montini, is crowned Pope Paul VI in Rome's St. Peter's Square.

Retreating From It All

24-year-old actress Dolores Hart gives up Hollywood and enters the Regina Laudis Monastery in Bethlehem, Connecticut as a postulant.

Pope John XXIII

THE PAPER CHASE

On the death of her husband, Philip Graham, Jr., chief executive officer of the WASHINGTON POST, Mrs. Katherine Meyer Graham succeeds her husband as publisher.

37-year-old Arthur Ochs Sulzberger takes over as president and publisher of the NEW YORK TIMES following the death of Orvil E. Dryfoos.

Harold Wilson is elected leader of the British Labour Party following the death of Hugh Gaitskell.

VICE ADMIRAL HYMAN G. RICKOVER, FATHER OF THE ATOMIC SUBMARINE, BOARDS THE ANDREW JACKSON, **FIRST NUCLEAR-POWERED SUBMARINE TO BE TESTED SINCE THE** THRESHER **DISASTER.**

PASSINGS

Civil rights activist, 37-year-old **Medgar Evers,** is shot and killed by Byron de la Beckwith while getting out of his car.

WILLIAM E. B. DuBOIS (95)

ELSA MAXWELL (80)

WIN A COOL SUMMER of barbecues, fun for the kids, or just lazing in the shade. Enter this great FLEXALUM CONTEST now. You can win a beautiful Flexalum Patio Cover–in the style and color you prefer–**CUSTOM-BUILT JUST FOR YOU.**

50 Custom-Built Flexalum Patio Covers–Values to $600 Each –Delivered and Installed Absolutely FREE to Homeowners.

Here's a checklist of some of the ways a guaranteed Flexalum® Patio Cover adds comfort, beauty and value to your home. Read it carefully. Pick the two features that are most important to you. Fill in the coupon and mail. There'll be a drawing from all entries and you may WIN a handsome, durable Flexalum Patio Cover–value up to $600–in your choice of colors and design–custom-built to fit the area you choose outside your house. Or, if you choose, the equivalent dollar value in Window Awnings.

Flexalum Patio Covers Give You : 1. Coolness—aluminum reflects heat away from you. 2. A new outdoor living room for the whole family. 3. An attractive and valuable addition to your home. 4. Two-coat baked enamel finish. 5. Heavy-gauge, spring-tempered aluminum construction. 6. A written, 5-year replacement guarantee, bonded by Continental Casualty Company, that the finish won't chip, peel or crack.

CONTEST RULES : A. The 50 (fifty) winners will be notified within two weeks of contest closing on March 31st, 1963. B. The winners must accept installation on their own homes within 60 days after notification. C. Only one free patio cover to a family. D. Your free patio cover will be built to cover up to 200 square feet (10' x 20'). You may specify dimensions subject to your dealer's engineering O.K. E. You can choose colors and striping. F. This contest is open to all homeowners in the United States. Subject to Federal, State and Local regulations. It is not open to employees of Bridgeport Brass, its dealers or advertising agencies.

Bridgeport Brass Company, Bridgeport, Connecticut

I am a homeowner.

My favorite Flexalum Patio Cover features are:

1   2   3   4   5   6   (circle two only)

Name_____

Address_____

City_____State_____

FLEXALUM manufacturers of Aluminum Siding, Awnings and Venetian Blinds for the home

Celebrating the 46th anniversary of the Bolshevik Revolution, Nikita Khrushchev makes the following comments:

"From a poor country we have come a long way to become the second country in the world. We give capitalism another seven years, then we will be first. Americans say Cuba is only 50 miles from their coast. But if the Americans attack Cuba, we shall attack America's allies, who are even closer to the Soviet Union. You are rejoicing that we are arguing with the Chinese, but the more pleased you feel now, the worse you will feel later on."

Commenting on an American Legion convention resolution asking the U.S. to "proceed boldly alone" against Cuba, President Kennedy says that he does not believe a U.S. military invasion of Cuba "is in the best interests of this country."

The Red Cross celebrates its 100th anniversary.

Nobel Peace Prize

Comité International de la Croix Rouge

International Committee of the Red Cross

Ligue des Sociétés de la Croix-Rouge

League of Red Cross Societies

1963

Blacks

The University of Alabama campus at Tuscaloosa is under a tight security guard of state police.

Governor George Wallace addresses the mob and appeals for calm as he prepares to confront a Deputy U.S. Attorney.

Federal officers arrive armed with a proclamation from President Kennedy urging the governor to end his efforts to prevent two black students from registering at the university.

The governor is adamant. He made a campaign promise to stand in the doorway himself to prevent integration of the last all-white state university.

WHAT A YEAR IT WAS!

Enrolled 1963

As Governor George Wallace Yields

After the federal officers leave (*left*), there is a lull of several hours while President Kennedy federalizes the Alabama National Guard and they move to the campus.

Brigadier General Henry Graham arrives to tell the governor: "It's my sad duty to ask you to step aside on orders of the president of the United States."

The governor yields to federal authority but promises to continue what he terms a constitutional fight. Wallace is escorted off campus and there is no violence during this confrontation of state and federal authorities.

WHAT A YEAR IT WAS!

CIVIL RIGHTS

Reverend Martin Luther King, Jr. launches new nonviolent campaign to end segregation.

30 PEOPLE ARRESTED in ALABAMA as violence erupts between blacks and police.

OVER 400 PEOPLE ARE ARRESTED and charged with trespass and disorderly conduct in BALTIMORE for demonstrating against the discriminatory practice of the Northwood movie theater. The theater management finally agrees to "admit all law-abiding persons."

1,000 PEOPLE ARRESTED in BIRMINGHAM in civil rights march.

POLICE, USING FIRE HOSES and dogs to disperse the crowd, arrest 500 people in BIRMINGHAM during black protest parade.

Police jail 600 black children in MISSISSIPPI.

450 BLACKS ARE ARRESTED in ALABAMA for defying injunction against sit-ins.

U.S. SUPREME COURT rules that cities in ALABAMA, LOUISIANA, NORTH CAROLINA and SOUTH CAROLINA can no longer use municipal ordinances to prosecute black Americans seeking service in privately owned stores, thus legalizing sit-ins as a means of enforcing desegregation.

OVER 1,400 BLACKS ARE ARRESTED and released pending trial in DURHAM, NORTH CAROLINA following mass demonstrations for desegregated public facilities.

WHAT A YEAR IT WAS!

STRUGGLE

MISSISSIPPI GOVERNOR Ross Barnett accuses President Kennedy of aiding the Communist plot to divide the U.S. through racial strife.

JEWISH, **PROTESTANT** and **CATHOLIC** clergymen along with Rev. Eugene Carson Blake are arrested in Baltimore protesting an all-white amusement park.

PRESIDENT KENNEDY says he opposes job quotas based on race.

In a television appearance, Rev. Martin Luther King, Jr., James Baldwin and Malcolm X call President Kennedy's leadership on civil rights inadequate.

Malcolm X

FOUR YOUNG BLACK GIRLS ARE KILLED AS A BOMB EXPLODES DURING A SUNDAY CHURCH SERVICE IN BIRMINGHAM, ALABAMA.

TWO MEN ARE ARRESTED IN CONNECTION WITH THE CHURCH BOMBING IN BIRMINGHAM.

A Test He's Bound To Fail
In a test of the housing discrimination ban, developer William Levitt refuses to sell plots to blacks.

Still The Struggle Continues

To commemorate the 100th anniversary of the Gettysburg Address, former President Eisenhower rededicates the Gettysburg cemetery.

And Finally...

According to a Gallup Poll, 83% of Southern blacks and whites answer "YES" to the following question:

"Do you think the day will ever come in the South when whites and blacks will be going to the same schools, eating in the same restaurants and generally sharing the same public accommodations?"

Dwight D. Eisenhower

1963

SEPARATION OF CHURCH AND STATE

The Supreme Court holds that state and local rules requiring recitation of the Lord's Prayer or of verses from the Bible in U.S. public schools violate the First Amendment's command that "Congress or any other agency of government shall make no law respecting an establishment of religion or prohibiting the free exercise thereof."

A SABBATH ON ANY OTHER DAY IS STILL A SABBATH

The Supreme Court rules unconstitutional a state's denial of unemployment compensation to an employee who refused to work on a particular day in observance of his Sabbath.

WAY TO GO, PAT!

California's Governor Edmund Brown signs a state code of fair practices prohibiting racial or religious discrimination by the state government and its outside contractors.

STUDY BY SMITH COLLEGE

CATHOLICS hold most extreme view on politics:
Anti-Castro 🏛 Anti-Soviet 🏛 Anti-Communist 🏛 Favor building fallout shelters 🏛 Have less information and hold strongly to a single point of view

PROTESTANTS, JEWS, UNITARIANS, ATHEISTS
hold less rigid views, see all sides of an issue and are less likely to view the world in terms of black and white

CATHOLICS & JEWS
who are Democrats hold vastly differing views on international affairs

How Very "Sheik" Of Them

The U.S. Defense Department reports that the Saudi Arabian government has lifted its ban against Jewish servicemen and is now permitting them to be stationed there. U.S. Jewish diplomats, congressmen, businessmen and tourists had also been barred from that country.

BACK IN THE CHURCH'S GOOD GRACES

After eight years of being excommunicated, the Vatican absolves **Juan Perón**.

In an unprecedented move, the pope admits five women as delegates to Vatican II.

ROME SPEAKS
Elizabeth Seton becomes the first American to become beatified.

NEWPORT, RHODE ISLAND'S TOURO SYNAGOGUE, THE OLDEST IN THE UNITED STATES, MARKS ITS BICENTENNIAL.

B'nai B'rith, the oldest Jewish service organization in the world, celebrates its 120th anniversary.

Celebrating its 50th anniversary, the Anti-Defamation League of B'nai B'rith presents President John F. Kennedy with its Democratic Legacy Award.

The Jewish Publication Society of America publishes a new translation of the Torah based on Masoretic (traditional Hebrew).

World Jewish population totals almost 13 million, with major concentrations as follows:

United States	5,500,000
U.S.S.R.	2,268,000
Israel	2,045,000

WHAT A YEAR IT WAS!

1963 STATISTICS

SCHOOL ENROLLMENT is up 44.6% from the 1952-53 school year.

HAVE PASSPORT – WILL TRAVEL

Visitors to the U.S. have increased 21.7% over last year while a record number of Americans have passports issued or renewed.

POPULATION

WORLD POPULATION	BIRTHRATE:
3.18 Billion	HIGHEST: Africa
	LOWEST: Europe (excluding the Soviet Union)

U.S. POPULATION
190,000,000

76% of the U.S. population has some form of health and accident insurance.

GO WEST, YOUNG MEN (AND WOMEN)–AND THEY DID!

California passes New York as the most populous state in America.

The U.S. Labor Department reports that for the first time the average factory wage tops $100 per week.

U.S. unemployment reaches 6.1%.

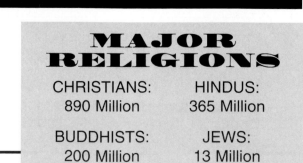

MAJOR RELIGIONS

CHRISTIANS: 890 Million	HINDUS: 365 Million
BUDDHISTS: 200 Million	JEWS: 13 Million

WOMEN, LOVE & Marriage
AND THE WHOLE DARN THING

- A majority of American women marry young and almost all women marry at least once.

- 1.6 million will marry this year.

- 400,000 women will divorce this year.

- One-third of all wives are working, with 42% of them with children between 6 and 18.

- Women take jobs early, quit when they have their first child and return to the workforce a few years later.

- Married women in their early 30s average well over three children.

- 65% are married by age 21.

- Many women have children before they're married with one out of every 20 babies born out of wedlock.

- Families prefer two to four children.

- There are almost two million divorced women in the country.

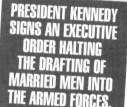

PRESIDENT KENNEDY SIGNS AN EXECUTIVE ORDER HALTING THE DRAFTING OF MARRIED MEN INTO THE ARMED FORCES.

NO PLACE LIKE HOME

According to a report from the Presidential Commission on the Status of Women, the modern homemaker's challenge is to see that her family has "a place where all members … can find acceptance, refreshment, self-esteem and renewal of strength amidst the pressures of modern life."

WHAT A YEAR IT WAS!

WOMEN OF AMERICA

UNITE!

PRESIDENT JOHN F. KENNEDY meets with 300 leaders of 93 organizations representing about 50 million women in an effort to win support for his rights program and to enlist their support in such efforts as:

a. ENCOURAGING CHILDREN to stay in school at least through high school.

b. SETTING UP LEADERSHIP courses in which women would be taught to fight prejudice.

c. COOPERATING with community biracial human relations committees that encourage contact between the white and black communities.

MISS U.S.A.	AMERICAN MOTHER OF THE YEAR
Marite Ozers (Miss Illinois)	**Olga Peterson Engdahl** (Omaha, Nebraska)
MISS AMERICA **Jacquelyn Mayer** (Sandusky, Ohio)	

WOMEN KNEW THIS ALL THE TIME

According to a professor at Harvard University, man's brain appears not to have increased in size since Neanderthal times, over 100,000 years ago, and in fact, may be shrinking in size.

WHAT A YEAR IT WAS!

AMERICAN WEEKLY, the oldest Sunday newspaper supplement in the U.S., ends publication.

The End Of A Tabloid

The New York **MIRROR** ends publication.

THE WOMEN'S NATIONAL PRESS CLUB establishes the **Eleanor Roosevelt Memorial Award** for women who make an outstanding contribution in the field of humanitarianism.

AND THESE ARE THEIR GOOD POINTS

Parade, a Sunday newspaper supplement, runs an article written by Jack Anderson entitled "Congressmen Who Cheat," charging that many members of Congress misuse government funds, pad their congressional payrolls and peddle influence.

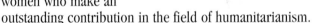

NATIONAL GEOGRAPHIC SOCIETY commemorates its 75th anniversary and opens new headquarters in Washington, D.C.

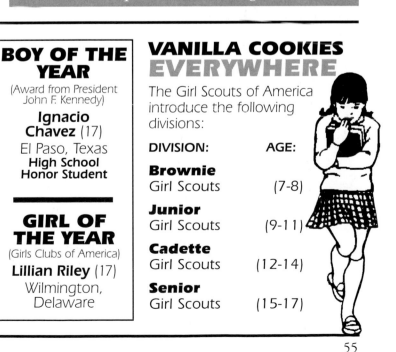

BOY OF THE YEAR
(Award from President John F. Kennedy)
Ignacio Chavez (17)
El Paso, Texas
High School Honor Student

GIRL OF THE YEAR
(Girls Clubs of America)
Lillian Riley (17)
Wilmington, Delaware

VANILLA COOKIES EVERYWHERE

The Girl Scouts of America introduce the following divisions:

DIVISION:	AGE:
Brownie Girl Scouts	(7-8)
Junior Girl Scouts	(9-11)
Cadette Girl Scouts	(12-14)
Senior Girl Scouts	(15-17)

GREAT TO GIVE, GRAND TO GET—WESTCLOX
Exclusive Drowse feature wakes you gently, lets you select 5 or 10 minutes' extra sleep, wakes you again. Electric alarm has smart beige case. $5.98. Trav-alarm has non-breakable case with sliding shutter front, easel back, luminous dial and bell alarm. $7.98

MUSICAL PLAYMATES FROM COLUMBIA TOY
These soft, fluffy nursery friends have built-in key-wound music boxes, satin ribbon bows. Wistful panda moves his eyes...perky poodle wears simulated pearl collar...sleepy-eyed puppy dog has soft felt tongue, floppy ears. Each for only $3.33
Manufactured by Columbia Toy Products, Inc. of Kansas City, Mo.

FITTING GIFTS—WATCHBANDS BY TOPPS
Handsome men's expansion bands come in beautiful stainless steel, or gleaming gold-finish with stainless steel backs. "Spring-bar" ends fit big watches, small watches, all watches in between. Choice of fashionable styles, yours for just $2.49

WESTINGHOUSE CLOCK-RADIO
The superb "Wake-To-Music" combines an accurate, easy-to-read electric clock with a wide-range, full-sound radio. Clock's "doze control" lets you catch extra sleep, wakes you again. In attractive full-molded cabinet. Give the "Wake-To-Music"!

WRAP UP YOUR

Santa's Specials

BUBBLE BATH
"Lisa Lane." Highly concentrated, delightfully fragrant. Luxurious! **69¢**

HOLIDAY CANDLES
Table decor! Brass feet, wooden stems, colored-glass holders. **69¢**

TREE LIGHT SET
8 lights. Bright colors. Tested, guaranteed sets. U.L. approved. **59¢**

FOSTORIA CORN POPPER POPS UP A STORM
Keep the popcorn coming, this gay party season. Pop all you need *fast* with this hefty, 4-quart popper. Durable aluminum stove, pan, lid; insulated bakelite handle; *plus* recipe book and supply of "Jolly Time" popcorn. Enjoy a Fostoria "instant" party for $5.95

ELECTREX WATERPROOF HEATING PAD
A particularly thoughtful gift, the Electrex Deluxe has an exclusive Sanifresh® bacteria-resistant quilted satin cover...six positive heats...Therma-Dial heat control unit with convenient Nite-Lite, and it comes guaranteed for four full years. $8.95

TIMEX...THE TORTURE-TESTED WATCH ON TV
You've seen its superior qualities proved! Give the beautiful shock-resistant Cavatina ladies' watch, or the smart men's Marlin shock-resistant; waterproof*; dustproof*. More people buy Timex than any other watch in the world! From $9.95 plus tax.
As long as crystal, crown and back are intact.

HERE'S MR. BIM AND SANTA, TOO!
It's love at first sight, when you see irresistible Mr. Bim! He's the monkey who hangs by his amazing "hold-on" hand from doorways, bookshelves—or anywhere you put him. $3.99. Santa Sock has zipper-back, makes a tote-bag for tots. Just $1.99
Manufactured by Columbia Toy Products, Inc. of Kansas City, Mo.

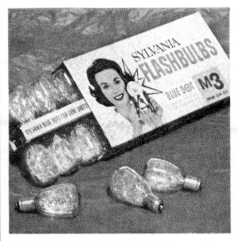

CAPTURE ALL THE HOLIDAY FUN
Christmas morning...holiday parties...they're all yours forever, in snapshots made with Sylvania flashbulbs. That little Blue Dot on each Sylvania flashbulb tells you it's good *before* you use it. Get Sylvania Blue Dots—world's most popular brand.

FULLY AUTOMATIC ELECTRIC BLANKET
A gift to be treasured for years! Beautiful blend modern luxury blanket fibers. 100% nylon Sanifres bacteria-resistant binding. Fashion-formed fc snug fit. Handy heat control dial lights in the da U.L. approved. Comes with 2-year guarantee. $18

GIFT LIST AT REXALL

YOUR Rexall STORE

This advertisement is presented on behalf of more than 10,000 independent pharmacists who recommend and feature products bearing the brand of the Rexall Drug Company. These suggested retail prices are effective through December 31, 1963, and are subject to Federal Excise Tax and other taxes as applicable. Right reserved to limit quantities, subject to compliance with applicable laws. Rexall Drug Co., Los Angeles 54, California. Satisfaction guaranteed or your money back.

ICICLES
Fireproof Revere foil. Each carton contains 75 strands. A "must"! **5¢**

VINYL TREE
3' high beauty has feathery "needles," sturdy steel tree stand. **$1⁷⁷**

GIVE THE LUXURY OF FINE AMITY LEATH
Masterfully-crafted of genuine leather, Am treasures make superb gifts: FOR HER, a Frer purse...roomy and regally lovely; FOR HIM Director billfold...sleek, slender, sumptuo Choose elegant Amity gifts, from $3.95 to $25
plus F.E.T.

MAKE YOUR HOME A WINTER WONDERLAND!
This holiday season, decorate with Spray Script and Crystal Frost. Use Spray Script to print—write —or draw holiday greetings on windows and glass doors...Crystal Frost to create frost-like patterns of dazzling beauty. Convenient spray-cans, each 98¢

STAINLESS ALUMINUM CHRISTMAS TREE
Standing a full six feet high, your shimmering silver tree will be a thing of beauty—always! Branches have gay pom-pom ends. Tree is fireproof, comes with its own metal stand. Tree dismantles for easy storage. This timeless Christmas buy, just $11.88

ELEGANT BRUSH AND COMB SETS
Men's and women's styles in beautiful antique g Brushes come in extra-stiff imported natural brist or the new tri-crimped nylon that pampers, polis the hair. Set includes matching comb and jew tray. Glamourous grooming gifts, from $2.00 to $

1963

SCRAPING THE SKY

The largest commercial office building in the world, the $100 million 59-story Pan Am Building, is completed in New York.

SPEED PAVING

A contractor in western Kentucky pours 2 miles of concrete in a single day, beating the previous record of just over 1 1/2 miles.

TRYING TO SAVE IT FROM THE WRECKING BALL

In an attempt to save this historic structure from being demolished, prominent architects picket New York's Pennsylvania Station.

Construction begins along St. Louis' waterfront on the 630-foot-high "Gateway Arch," designed by the late Eero Saarinen, which on completion will be the nation's tallest monument.

What's Yale Have To Say About This?

The first U.S. building by world-famous architect Le Corbusier is completed at Harvard University.

Is There A Midget In There Or What?

New Yorkers are startled as a talking garbage can called "Lively Louie," installed in New York's Times Square, tells them that "A cleaner New York is up to you!"

U.S. Supreme Court dismisses a plea to block the proposed construction of the World Trade Center in New York.

Honey, I'm Home – Where's My Gun?

California drivers going home from work using the freeways are under more stress than an astronaut in orbit, according to tests conducted using an Air Force bio-measuring device.

THE U.S. SENATE passes a bill requiring that automobile seat belts sold or shipped in interstate commerce meet certain safety standards.

Buckle Up For Safety – All The Time

Accident data collected for over a year in Michigan shows that seat belts are most effective in city driving and that nearly one-third of the 70 deaths could have been avoided if a seat belt had been worn.

Hard To Teach Bad Drivers New Tricks

Dr. James L. Malfetti of Columbia University concludes that safety education films packed with gore don't scare bad drivers into becoming better drivers as evidenced by drivers who, after watching these films, went out and drove exactly the same way they had been before.

Tell Us How You Felt As You Ran Over His Face

The New York Department of Traffic has called in the Postgraduate Center for Mental Health to devise a mass psychology in an attempt to reduce the number of deadly accidents.

THE CHIMP DIDN'T GET BUSTED
A carnival showman is arrested in Tampa, Florida and charged with reckless driving for allowing his chimpanzee to drive his car at 70 miles per hour on a local highway.

There's Mary Ann, Mary Catherine, Mary Margaret and...James Andrew

Andrew and Mary Ann Brady Fischer of Aberdeen, South Dakota produce the first U.S. quintuplets to survive early infancy.

Let's Put Some Limits on Dividing and Multiplying

The National Academy of Sciences proposes that the U.S. government actively participate in encouraging international birth control studies.

The Ford Foundation announces grants totaling over $5,000,000 for birth control aid to underdeveloped countries.

ACCORDING TO A REPORT RELEASED BY PRESIDENT KENNEDY'S COUNCIL ON AGING, NEARLY 18 MILLION AMERICANS 65 YEARS OR OLDER HAVE COME DANGEROUSLY CLOSE TO BECOMING SECOND-CLASS CITIZENS.

THE ADVISORY COMMISSION ON NARCOTIC & DRUG ABUSE

submits a report to President Kennedy with the following recommendations:

- **Launch a massive attack against importers and big distributors of narcotics.**
- **Place strict controls on drugs that have potential for abuse that could cause psychotic or antisocial behavior.**
- **Relax criminal sanctions for illegal drug use and increase government funding of medical and psychological research into the underlying causes of drug abuse.**

New Hampshire legalizes nation's only sweepstakes.

Hugh Hefner

is found not guilty in an obscenity trial against PLAYBOY for publishing boudoir photographs of actress Jayne Mansfield.

An Attorney For Everyone

The Supreme Court reverses itself, holding that states must provide free counsel for indigents facing serious criminal charges.

WHEN ONE SPEAKS, THEY ALL LISTEN

In the nation's first educational computer network, western institutions are linked together through the Western Data Processing Center and include:

California Institute of Technology
University of California at San Diego
Stanford University
U.S. Air Force Academy
University of Southern California
University of Utah

Double-Decker Desks?

President Kennedy's "Special Message on Education" stresses the problems of shortage of teachers and classrooms.

They Must Miss That Great Cafeteria Food

A report from the National Opinion Research Center reveals that 25 million adult Americans are involved in some type of continuing education classes.

President Kennedy visits Vanderbilt University in Nashville for the school's 90th anniversary celebration.

1963

THE HIGH COST OF MAILING A LETTER

U.S. Post Office raises postage for first-class stamps to 5¢.

U.S. postmaster general introduces zip codes.

✓ DOES THIS INCLUDE TICKETS FOR THE N.Y. KNICKS?

The IRS issues its final, more liberalized rules on the new expense account tax deductions which allow deductions without proof of actual business dealings for:

a. Meals and drinks in quiet surroundings conducive to business discussions.

b. Entertaining in a clear business setting such as a "hospitality room" for a business convention or a party celebrating the opening of a hotel.

Life's More Fun Above The Ground

In a study conducted at Michigan State University, it is discovered that most Americans would rather be "Red Than Dead" vs. the popularly held slogan "Better Dead Than Red."

Plant Your Feet Here For A While

The Garden Club of America holds it 50th annual meeting in Philadelphia.

Nuke Those Little Suckers

The Food and Drug Administration considers approving the use of radiation to kill insects in wheat and wheat products.

GENERAL MILLS DEVELOPS GRANULAR FLOUR THAT POURS LIKE SUGAR.

THAT'S A LOT OF OF BREAD

In the largest commercial transaction ever made between the U.S. and the U.S.S.R., President Kennedy authorizes the sale of more than $250 million worth of U.S. wheat and wheat flour.

20-year-old dairy farmer
Robert A. Cummins
of Warsaw, N.Y. is named
the Star Farmer of America.

GETTING BIG BUCKS FOR THEIR POUND OF FLESH

The winner of the 64th annual International Livestock Exposition in Chicago is a 950-pound Hereford steer named "**Real McCoy**," who is sold the next day at a public auction for $10 a pound, almost double what last year's winner sold for.

A Word Or Two From Lizzie's Company

THE BORDEN COMPANY brings out 35 new products including an instant omelet mix, imitation cream with low-fat content, dehydrated sweet-potato flakes and mushroom chips for cocktail snacks.

WHAT A YEAR IT WAS!

JESSE JAMES
RIDES AGAIN (ENGLISH STYLE)

In the biggest armed robbery ever carried out in Great Britain, a gang of 20 armed masked robbers halts and robs a train, heading from Glasgow to London, of more than $7 million.

NEVER TOO LATE FOR JUSTICE

An alleged aide of the late Adolf Eichmann, Austrian-born Erich Rajakovich, surrenders to Austrian authorities in Vienna to face charges of sending thousands of Jews to their death in Nazi-occupied Austria, Belgium and the Netherlands during World War II.

This Zoo Has Full TRUNKS

Two more Indian elephants are born at the Portland, Oregon Zoo, bringing the total at that zoo to four baby elephants in just 18 months.

BULGARIA, CZECHOSLOVAKIA, HUNGARY, POLAND and ROMANIA – NYEt

Citing national security, travel restrictions are placed on diplomats of five Soviet-bloc countries by the U.S. State Department.

what! NO BELUGA CAVIAR??

22 cities in the U.S. enact ordinances prohibiting or discouraging the sale by local merchants of products made in the Soviet Union and its satellites.

1963

GET UNDER A DESK, PUT YOUR HEAD BETWEEN YOUR LEGS AND KISS YOUR TUSH GOOD-BYE

Police in England seize copies of pamphlets from demonstrators during an anti-nuclear weapons rally purported to reveal the British government's plans for reorganization in case of nuclear war.

YOU KNOW THE DRILL — GET UNDER THE DESK, ETC., ETC.

Citing its uselessness in the event of a nuclear war, Portland, Oregon disbands its civil defense program.

70,000 MARCH IN A-BOMB PROTEST IN LONDON.

President Kennedy asks Congress to abolish IMMIGRATION QUOTAS.

West Germany reports that over 16,000 people have escaped from the East in the two years since the Berlin Wall went up.

THEY'RE DREAMING OF A "WEST" CHRISTMAS

Under the 17-day Christmas accord, 4,000 people cross the Berlin Wall to visit relatives.

WHAT? NO RICE?

Following their wedding, 1,000 Londoners throw eggs at British Nazi leader Colin Jordan and his new wife.

BRRRR

The coldest January and February since 1740 strikes Britain.

JUST WHEN THEY WERE PERFECTING THEIR BACKSTROKES

Alcatraz, the infamous prison in San Francisco Bay that housed Al Capone along with some of the most incorrigible prisoners in the federal prison system, closes down due to its deterioration.

"UP, UP & AWAY, IN MY BEAUTIFUL... AIRPLANE"

AMERICANS DON PICCARD and ED YOST are the first to cross the English Channel in a hot air balloon.

 Piloted by Col. James B. Swindal, the fan jet Boeing 707-320B assigned to President Kennedy, who is not on board, breaks 15 speed records by flying nonstop 5,002 miles from Washington to Moscow in 8 hours, 38 minutes, 42 seconds at an average speed of 580 mph.

37-year-old aviatrix Betty Miller of Santa Monica, California becomes first woman pilot to fly solo over the Pacific from California to Australia.

Piloting an X-15 experimental rocket plane released from its B-52 mother craft, Joseph Walker sets a new altitude record of 354,200 feet, or over 67 miles.

Aviatrix Jacqueline Cochran flies at a speed of 1,273.109 mph in a Lockheed F-104G jet.

RACING WOMEN...

The 13th Annual All-Women's International Air Race is won by Mrs. Bernice T. Steadman of Flint, Michigan.

The 17th Annual All-Woman Transcontinental Air Race is won by Virginia Britt with Lee Winfield as her copilot.

Is There A Doctor In The House?

According to the medical service of the Federal Aviation Agency, more than 50% of airplane accidents occur at or near airports and it is recommended that large airports beef up their medical facilities, which are presently insufficient.

James Whittaker plants an American flag on top of Mt. Everest, as he becomes the first American to conquer that formidable Himalayan peak.

BETTER GET OUT THOSE WOOLIES
In an expedition sponsored by the U.S. Air Force Office of Scientific Research, the largest party of scientists to explore the Arctic is assembled in Alaska.

INTERCONTINENTAL BOMBER SCORES
[NUMBER IN INVENTORY]

United States:	630
U.S.S.R.:	190

WHAT A YEAR IT WAS!

WATER...WATER...WATER

It Never Rains In Southern California, But It Sure Got Damp

The Baldwin Hills Dam in Los Angeles bursts sending a deluge of over 292,000,000 gallons of water into the suburban valley below.

FRANKLY, THEY GIVE A DAM

The U.S. Army Corps of Engineers is awarded its largest civil contract in history — $70,500,000 for a 2,000-foot powerhouse, a fish ladder and a non-overflow section at the John Day Dam in Washington.

Better Curb Your Thirst

A seven-man presidential task force on water resources reports that based on current conservation practices, 75% of the water in rivers and streams in the U.S. would have to be withdrawn to meet the nation's needs by the year 2000. 25% is currently being withdrawn.

Help Is On The Way

President Kennedy approves emergency aid to poverty-stricken people in eastern Kentucky's Appalachia region.

ARCHAEOLOGISTS IN NEWFOUNDLAND DISCOVER VIKING RUINS PREDATING COLUMBUS BY 500 YEARS.

ME GET BIG FURRY BEAST

An article in the JOURNAL OF THE AMERICAN MEDICAL ASSOCIATION asserts that hunters were probably history's first talkers.

WELL NOW, AIN'T THAT THE CAT'S MEOW

President of the American Veterinary Medical Association reports that dogs reflect the personalities of their owners, who are generally more interdependent with their pets, while cat owners are generally independent-minded and reject the idea of emotional dependence on pets or emotional involvement with them.

DID YOU HUG YOUR MONKEY PLAYMATE TODAY?

Studies conducted at the Wisconsin Regional Primate Center at Madison, Wisconsin on the importance of affection from playmates on the emotional development of young monkeys, reveal that female monkeys who are not adequately mothered turn out to be inadequate mothers themselves unless they obtain support and affection from playmates at an early age. Male monkeys deprived of affectionate relationships during infancy are more poorly adjusted than their female counterparts.

YOU'D BETTER HANG ON TIGHT

New evidence supports the theory of continental drift, which holds that the earth is an ever-changing planet upon which the continents drift and the North Pole shifts.

Let's Start With More Andy Gumps

President Kennedy signs a law establishing the Bureau of Outdoor Recreation, which will coordinate efforts to meet the demand for outdoor recreation facilities.

There's Diamonds In Them Thar Mines

Russian geologists discover new diamond deposits in Africa.

1963
TEEN CORNER

NO ONE LOVES A SMARTY PANTS

A study by the Talented Youth Project of the Horace Mann Lincoln Institute of School Experimentation reveals that teenagers distrust brilliant students and list the qualities of a popular student as follows:

- **Cheerful**
- **A Good Sport**
- **Nice Looking**
- **Good Leader**
  (but not a perfectionist)
- **Good Conversationalist**

REASONS FOR TEENAGE BAD EATING HABITS:

- Desire to gain weight to make the football team.
- Need for high food intake during the formative years.
- Have funds to snack at the neighborhood drugstore or drive-in.
- Overfed as babies and adolescents.
- Peer pressure – going along with the gang.

Education, YES! Quit School, NO!

President John F. Kennedy makes an appeal to school boards to take steps to halt the growth of youth unemployment and makes available a summer fund of $250,000 to be used to make a special effort to get potential dropouts back to school.

THE PRESIDENT'S COMMITTEE ON YOUTH EMPLOYMENT submits a report to President Kennedy warning that 600,000-800,000 young people between the ages of 16-21 are facing severe job problems and calls for "bold and imaginative action" to counter the growing youth unemployment problem.

THE CORPS

A jobs program including creation of the **YOUTH CONSERVATION CORPS** is proposed by President Kennedy.

President Kennedy submits a draft bill to Congress for the creation of a **National Service Corps** (domestic Peace Corps) which would be open to people of all ages who would receive living and travel costs plus a $75 monthly salary.

Television sales pass the $1,000,000,000 mark for the first time.

POPULAR ADVERTISING SLOGANS

"Come Alive! You're in the Pepsi generation."
(Pepsi-Cola)

"You don't have to be Jewish to love Levy's."
(Levy's Bread)

"Relieves gas pains."
(Volkswagen)

"A Different Breed of Cat."
(Jaguar XKE)

"Things Go Better with Coke."
(Coca-Cola)

"Open wide and say ahhh."
(National Library Week)

"When You're Only No. 2, You Try Harder. Or Else."
(Avis Rent-A-Car)

WHAT YOU SEE AIN'T NECESSARILY WHAT YOU GET

In response to public sentiment about misleading labeling practices, Senator Philip A. Hart of Michigan chairs a congressional subcommittee on deceptive packaging and labeling practices.

WHAT A YEAR IT WAS!

New Words & Expressions

Reprography
Duplication via a facsimile machine.

Aunt Jane
Black woman who believes in nonviolent civil rights protests.

MODERN Marches FOR JOBS & FREEDOM

Freedom Walker
One who walks to oppose racial prejudice.

Scubacide
When an inexpert scuba diver dies.

Automania
The desire to have a car for status.

FLIM-FLAM

Hospital Staph
Bacteria immune to many drugs.

Sherwood Forest
The large area on a ship for storing weapons.

Beatlemania
All things **Beatles** all the time.

Nitty-Gritty
The little details.

Pirt
Short pants worn under a skirt.

SMU
Self-maneuvering unit, a backpack which astronauts use in space to fix their spacecraft.

Space Docking
When two spaceships connect in outer space.

Bicycle Boulevard
Bicycle paths that run along main roads.

Plastinaut
An astronaut mannequin.

Eraserophagia
A mild ailment that results from ingesting pieces of an eraser.

Urbophrenia
Nervousness brought about by living in a contemporary metropolis.

Wallpaper Music
Another name for background music.

FROM 10 YEARS OF COLOR EXPERIENCE

Admiral brings three new major improvements to color television

1. Greater Dependability—with Gold Precision Wiring in the most vital areas. This quality advance —like the precision jewels in a fine watch—assures long, trouble-free life. And only Admiral has it! Using electro-deposition, Admiral applies 5 micro-inches of pure 24-karat gold to precision-wiring for the greatest dependability ever in the most vital areas of a color tv set.

2. More Natural Color—with Electronic Color Balancer. Now, enjoy the same natural color the camera sees! This new Admiral development brings you true-to-life beauty—and does it for you automatically! Unlike other color tv, new Admiral precision circuitry actually increases the power of *each* color signal *individually* and balances them for more natural color reproduction.

The all-new Admiral Color TV SP-26 Chassis... precision-crafted, 26,000 volts...24-hour life-tested for unmatched dependability

3. New Easier Tuning—with a new Color TV Contrast Control. No other color tv can be tuned as simply and as easily! Admiral ends unnecessary fumbling with controls. This Admiral "exclusive" automatically maintains eye-pleasing brightness as you adjust for proper contrast. It makes tuning simple and easy. And only Admiral Color tv has it!

See the complete selection of fine furniture—Contemporary, Danish Modern, Early American, French Provincial—handcrafted from genuine veneers and hardwood solids...at your quality Admiral Dealer.

Admiral "Sonar" full-function, wireless remote control turns tv on...changes channels...adjusts and mutes sound...turns tv completely off. Enjoy easy-chair tuning with great savings! Just $30.00*

ADMIRAL COLOR
MARK OF QUALITY THROUGHOUT THE WORLD

Shown above (left) The Chanceford, Model L1629, (right) The Courtney, Model L1311.   Admiral, Chicago. Canadian Admiral, Port Credit, Ont. *Prices and specifications subject to change without notice. UHF available, optional extra.

Arts & ENTERTAINMENT

MOVIES

GET OUT THOSE **BOOGIE BOARDS**

BEACH PARTY, starring **Annette Funicello, Frankie Avalon, Bob Cummings** and **Dorothy Malone,** plugs into the growing surfing craze.

BOB CUMMINGS
DOROTHY MALONE
FRANKIE AVALON
ANNETTE FUNICELLO
HARVEY LEMBECK
JODY McCREA
JOHN ASHLEY

It's what happens when 10,000 kids meet on 5,000 Beach Blankets!

AMSTERDAM and SIX

DICK DALE AND THE DEL TONES

BEACH PARTY

PATHECOLOR and PANAVISION

ASHER · RUSOFF · NICHOLSON · RUSOFF · ARKOFF · BAXTER

MUSIC

The Beatles' second U.K. single, "Please Please Me," backed with "Ask Me Why," reaches #1 on the British pop charts, making it their first #1 hit.

Paul McCartney, Ringo Starr, George Harrison, John Lennon

TELEVISION

Immediately following the assassination of President **John F. Kennedy**, all television and radio networks cancel their regular schedules and expand complete coverage to an unprecedented five days.

ART

NORMAN ROCKWELL paints the last of his 317 *Saturday Evening Post* **covers.**

What's Playing At THE MOVIES

THE CARDINAL
CHARADE
Children Of The Damned
Cleopatra
COME BLOW YOUR HORN
Come Fly With Me
FLIPPER
Follow The Boys
For Love Or Money
FROM RUSSIA WITH LOVE
Fun In Acapulco
Gidget Goes To Rome
THE GREAT ESCAPE
Greenwich Village Story
THE HAUNTED PALACE
THE HAUNTING
Hud
I Could Go On Singing
I Was A Teenage Thumb
In The Cool Of The Day

8 1/2
A Child Is Waiting
A Gathering Of Eagles
A STITCH IN TIME
All The Way Home
The Balcony
Beach Party
Billy Liar
THE BIRDS
BYE BYE BIRDIE

WHAT A YEAR IT WAS!

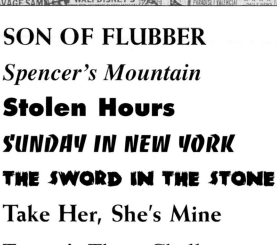

The Incredibly Strange Creatures Who Stopped Living And Became Mixed-Up Zombies

IRMA LA DOUCE
It Happened At The World's Fair
It's A Mad Mad Mad Mad World
Jason And The Argonauts
Kings Of The Sun
THE KISS OF THE VAMPIRE
Ladybug, Ladybug
LILIES OF THE FIELD
The List Of Adrian Messenger
LORD OF THE FLIES
Love With The Proper Stranger
MARY, MARY
Miracle Of The White Stallions
Move Over, Darling
THE NUTTY PROFESSOR
PT 109
The Servant
SHOCK CORRIDOR
Shotgun Wedding
The Skydivers
The Small World Of Sammy Lee
Soldier In The Rain

SON OF FLUBBER
Spencer's Mountain
Stolen Hours
SUNDAY IN NEW YORK
THE SWORD IN THE STONE
Take Her, She's Mine
Tarzan's Three Challenges
THIS SPORTING LIFE
The Three Stooges Go Around The World In A Daze
The Thrill Of It All
TOM JONES
TOYS IN THE ATTIC
Transylvania 6-5000
The Ugly American
UNDER THE YUM YUM TREE
THE V.I.P.S
The Victors
What's a Nice Girl Like You Doing In A Place Like This?
THE WHEELER DEALERS
Who's Been Sleeping In My Bed?

Golden Globe AWARDS

Next to the Oscars®, probably the most coveted awards in movie circles are the Golden Globes, which are bestowed by the Hollywood Foreign Press Association, and fans line up to catch a glimpse of their favorite stars.

GREGORY PECK *(left)* is being honored, as is the lovely DORIS DAY.

TONY RANDALL is among the early arrivals for the 20th Annual Ceremony.

Arriving with EDIE ADAMS, ROCK HUDSON is beseiged for autographs. Rock is another winner among the correspondents.

The cameras are first focused on Gregory Peck, who has received wide acclaim for his acting in the smash hit *To Kill A Mockingbird.*

JANE WYMAN presents the award to Rock Hudson, who is the male world film favorite. Rock has won this award three times.

And the evening ends on a beautiful note as Doris Day receives the award for the female world film favorite from CHARLTON HESTON.

There is an overflow crowd of more than 1,000 people in the Coconut Grove to applaud the winners in this global competition.

WHAT A YEAR IT WAS!

71

1963

The Academy Awards

"And The Winner Is..."

Oscars® Presented in 1963

BEST PICTURE
LAWRENCE OF ARABIA

BEST ACTOR
GREGORY PECK, *To Kill A Mockingbird*

BEST ACTRESS
ANNE BANCROFT, *The Miracle Worker*

BEST DIRECTOR
DAVID LEAN, *Lawrence Of Arabia*

BEST SUPPORTING ACTOR
ED BEGLEY, *Sweet Bird Of Youth*

BEST SUPPORTING ACTRESS
PATTY DUKE, *The Miracle Worker*

BEST SONG
"DAYS OF WINE AND ROSES," *Days Of Wine And Roses*

Gregory Peck finally wins an Oscar after being nominated five times.

16-year-old Patty Duke becomes the first performer under 18 to win a competitive Oscar.

Gregory Peck

1963 Favorites *(Oscars® Presented in 1964)*

BEST PICTURE
TOM JONES

BEST ACTOR
SIDNEY POITIER, *Lilies Of The Field*

BEST ACTRESS
PATRICIA NEAL, *Hud*

BEST DIRECTOR
TONY RICHARDSON, *Tom Jones*

BEST SUPPORTING ACTOR
MELVYN DOUGLAS, *Hud*

BEST SUPPORTING ACTRESS
MARGARET RUTHERFORD, *The V.I.P.s*

BEST SONG
"CALL ME IRRESPONSIBLE," *Papa's Delicate Condition*

Sidney Poitier

WHAT A YEAR IT WAS!

SINGING AND COMEDY TONIGHT

Frank Sinatra replaces **Bob Hope** as host of the Academy Awards ceremony when the comedian's regular television sponsors conflict with the Academy's.

Frank Sinatra becomes special assistant to **Jack L. Warner**, president of Warner Bros.

A Tasty Morsel

Hollywood film star 28-year-old Shirley MacLaine is chosen Woman of the Year by Harvard's Hasty Pudding Club.

MUSIC TO HIS EARS

74-year-old composer Irving Berlin is awarded the Milestone Award of the Screen Producers Guild.

WINNER

New York Film Critics Award

Albert Finney
(Tom Jones)

CAN YOU HUM THE FIRST THREE BARS?

For the first time, the five songs nominated for an Oscar are presented in a medley.

The $17,000,000 film version of *My Fair Lady*, the costliest film made in Hollywood, nears completion at year-end.

WHAT A YEAR IT WAS!

Photoplay

Among the winners of this year's coveted Photoplay Awards are **Gary Clarke** *(left)*, **Suzanne Pleshette** and **Richard Chamberlain**.

Suzanne's choice as most promising actress gets the approval of **Sebastian Cabot** *(top right)* as well as **Johnny Carson** *(bottom)* and others at the New York gold medal party.

Hailed as best actress is **Bette Davis** *(right, in photo at left)*, seated with **Hedda Hopper**.

Virginian star Gary Clarke shares cutting-the-cake honors with Suzanne Pleshette.

The proud winners display their awards.

WHAT A YEAR IT WAS!

Now—get color pictures in 50 seconds with the world's most advanced camera

Everywhere, reaction to Polaroid 50-second color film has been exciting. The colors are rich and clear. Skin tones are remarkably accurate. And it's difficult *not* to get excited about seeing color pictures 50 seconds after you take them.

Now Polaroid introduces a camera designed to take maximum advantage of the astonishing new Polacolor film. The Polaroid Color Pack Camera is the most advanced camera in the world. Because it has a transistorized shutter, it can do things no camera could ever do before. You can shoot color indoors without special settings or flash guides (the electric eye reads the flash and sets the exposure automatically). You can shoot black and white in low light levels (a candlelit dinner table, for instance) and the shutter will automatically make the correct setting for a time exposure.

The camera is easy to use. It's also lighter than many 35mm cameras. The film comes in a pack that loads in 7 seconds. Let your dealer show you how the world's most advanced camera makes picture-taking more fun than ever.

75

Famous BIRTHS

Johnny Depp
Helen Hunt
Greg Kinnear
Jet Li
Dermot Mulroney
Mike Myers
Tatum O'Neal
Brad Pitt
Natasha Richardson
Elisabeth Shue
Steven Soderbergh
Quentin Tarantino
Jeanne Tripplehorn
Vanessa Williams

Passings

John Farrow (58)
Adolphe Menjou (73)
Zasu Pitts (65)
Jason Robards, Sr. (70)
Sabu (39)

Dick Powell (58)

ANDY WARHOL PRODUCTIONS
(Producer/Director)

- - - - - - - -

Kiss
Eat
Sleep
Haircut

In Bangkok for the opening of *The Ugly American*, **Marlon Brando** discusses Buddhism with Thailand's King Bhumibol.

President Kennedy selects **Cliff Robertson** to portray him in the movie *PT 109*, based on the president's World War II heroic efforts for which he received the Purple Heart and the Navy and Marine Corps Medal for his bravery.

DON'T TAKE IT OFF — DON'T TAKE IT ALL OFF

DANA ANDREWS, new president of the Screen Actors Guild, denounces nudity in films.

HONK NO MORE

Horn-honking **Harpo Marx** breaks his 45 years of "silence" to announce his retirement from show business.

WHAT A YEAR IT WAS!

TOP TEN
BOX OFFICE STARS

1963

Doris Day

Cary Grant

Doris Day
Sandra Dee
Cary Grant
Rock Hudson
Jack Lemmon
Jerry Lewis
Paul Newman
Elvis Presley
Elizabeth Taylor
John Wayne

Jerry Lewis

STARS
OF TOMORROW

Ursula Andress
Tony Bill
George Chakiris
Barbara Eden
Peter Fonda
Diane McBain
Dorothy Provine
Pamela Tiffin
Pat Wayne

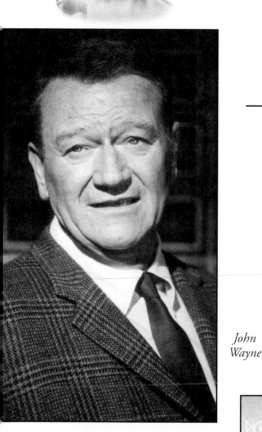

John Wayne

Ursula Andress

Peter Fonda

TOP
MONEYMAKER OF THE YEAR
CLEOPATRA

FLOP
OF THE YEAR
CLEOPATRA

WHAT A YEAR IT WAS!

now it's Pepsi-for those who <u>think</u> <u>young</u>

When today's active people stop to refresh, the refreshment they go for is Pepsi! Light, bracing Pepsi-Cola matches your modern activities with a sparkling-clean taste that's never too sugary or sweet. Nothing drenches your thirst like a cold, inviting Pepsi. Think young—say "Pepsi, please!"

PEPSI-COLA

TELEVISION 1963

What's On TV This Week
- a sampling -

The Adventures Of Ozzie And Harriet
The Alfred Hitchcock Hour
The Andy Griffith Show
The Andy Williams Show
Armstrong Circle Theater*
Ben Casey
The Beverly Hillbillies
Bonanza
Breaking Point
Car 54, Where Are You?*
Cheyenne*
Combat
The Danny Thomas Show
The Defenders
Dennis The Menace*
The Dick Powell Show*
The Dick Van Dyke Show
The Dinah Shore Chevy Show*
The Donna Reed Show
Dr. Kildare
The Ed Sullivan Show
Eyewitness To History*
Father Knows Best*
The Garry Moore Show
Going My Way*

Gunsmoke
Have Gun Will Travel*
Hawaiian Eye*
Hazel
I'm Dickens, He's Fenster*
I've Got A Secret
The Jack Benny Program
The Jack Paar Program
Jackie Gleason And His American Scene Magazine
The Jetsons*
Laramie*
Lassie
The Lawrence Welk Show
Leave It To Beaver*
The Lloyd Bridges Show*
The Lucy Show
Make That Spare
The Many Loves Of Dobie Gillis*
McHale's Navy
Meet The Press
Mister Ed
Mr. Smith Goes To Washington*
My Three Sons

Naked City*
The New Loretta Young Show*
The Nurses
Our Man Higgins*
Password
The Perry Como Show*
Perry Mason
The Price Is Right
Rawhide
The Real McCoys*
The Red Skelton Show
The Rifleman*
Route 66
77 Sunset Strip
Sing Along With Mitch
Stump The Stars*
To Tell The Truth
The Twilight Zone
The Untouchables*
The Virginian
Wagon Train
Walt Disney's Wonderful World Of Color
What's My Line?

*Final Season

WHAT A YEAR IT WAS!

AND FOR THE VERY FIRST TIME...

Bob Hope Presents The Chrysler Theater
Burke's Law
The Danny Kaye Show
East Side/West Side
The Farmer's Daughter
The Fugitive
General Hospital
Glynis
The Great Adventure
The Greatest Show On Earth
Hollywood And The Stars
Hootenanny
The Judy Garland Show
Let's Make A Deal
The Lieutenant
Mr. Novak
My Favorite Martian
The New Phil Silvers Show
The Outer Limits
The Patty Duke Show
Petticoat Junction
The Richard Boone Show
The Sid Caesar Show
Temple Houston

My Favorite Martian's
Ray Walston

Danny Kaye

Judy Garland &
Phil Silvers

Sid Caesar

WINTER
TOP RATED SHOWS

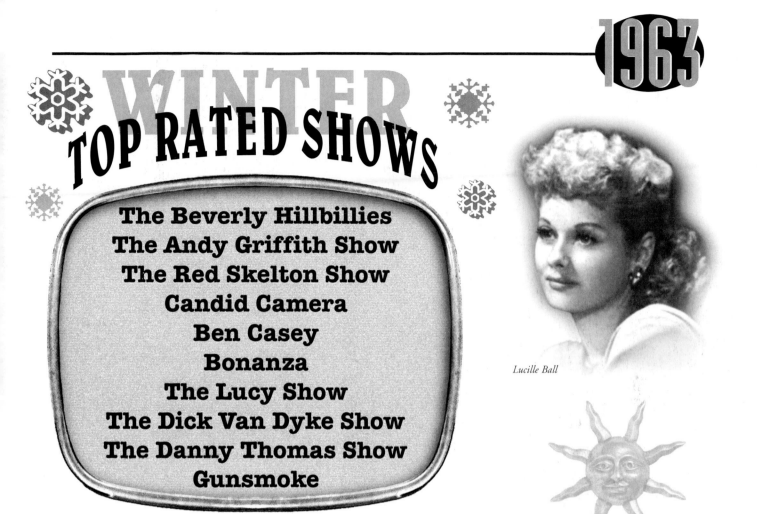

The Beverly Hillbillies
The Andy Griffith Show
The Red Skelton Show
Candid Camera
Ben Casey
Bonanza
The Lucy Show
The Dick Van Dyke Show
The Danny Thomas Show
Gunsmoke

Lucille Ball

SUMMER
TOP RATED SHOWS

Beverly Hillbilly
Buddy Ebsen

Miss America Pageant
The Beverly Hillbillies
The Dick Van Dyke Show
Gunsmoke
Bonanza
Vacation Playhouse
Grindl
What's My Line?
Walt Disney's Wonderful
World of Color

WHAT A YEAR IT WAS!

1963
FACES SEEN ON THE

Bill Bixby

Joseph Cotten

Don Adams
Edie Adams
Eddie "Rochester" Anderson
Desi Arnaz
Fred Astaire
John Astin
Lucille Ball
Ralph Bellamy
Bill Bixby
Dan Blocker
Ernest Borgnine
Walter Brennan
David Brinkley
Raymond Burr
Edd "Kookie" Byrnes
Angela Cartwright
Richard Chamberlain
Lee J. Cobb
Imogene Coca
Chuck Connors
Tim Conway
Joseph Cotten
Bob Crane
Johnny Crawford
Richard Crenna
Vic Damone
Ann B. Davis
Bob Denver
Bruce Dern
Troy Donahue
Clint Eastwood

Buddy Ebsen
Chad Everett
Shelley Fabares
Joe Flynn
James Franciscus
William Frawley
Ben Gazzara
Alice Ghostley
Gale Gordon
Lorne Greene
Shecky Greene
Merv Griffin
Fred Gwynne
Pat Harrington, Jr.
Earl Holliman
Ronny Howard
Chet Huntley
David Janssen
Gene Kelly
Don Knotts
Michael Landon
Jerry Lewis
Jack Lord
Allen Ludden
Gavin MacLeod
Fred MacMurray
Meredith MacRae
E. G. Marshall
Jerry Mathers
Martin Milner
Candy Moore

Meredith MacRae

Shelley Fabares

82

WHAT A YEAR IT WAS!

BOOB TUBE

Rod Serling

Mary Tyler Moore
Harry Morgan
Jim Nabors
Ryan O'Neal
The Osmond Brothers
Jack Palance
Fess Parker
Robert Reed
Carl Reiner
Burt Reynolds
Mickey Rooney
Marion Ross
Kurt Russell
George C. Scott
Rod Serling
Howard K. Smith
Robert Stack
Connie Stevens
Cicely Tyson
Leslie Uggams
Vivian Vance
Jerry Van Dyke
Mike Wallace
Ray Walston
Dennis Weaver
Jane Wyatt
Dick York
Robert Young

Jane Wyatt

GUN SMOKOVICH

The Soviets celebrate the 25th anniversary of television in the U.S.S.R.

The Soviets shut down NBC's Moscow news bureau in retaliation for what it calls broadcasts that *"grossly distorted Soviet reality and had the obvious purpose of arousing...hostile sentiments against the Soviet Union."*

Washington, D.C.'s WOOK-TV is the first all-black TV station in the U.S.

"Vast wasteland" Newton Minow resigns as head of the FCC.

SERIES

Humor
The Dick Van Dyke Show

Drama
The Defenders

Variety
The Andy Williams Show

Music
Julie And Carol At Carnegie Hall

News Report
The Huntley-Brinkley Report

Program Of The Year
The Tunnel

ENTERTAINERS

Actor	**E. G. Marshall** *The Defenders*
Actress	**Shirley Booth** *Hazel*
Performer (Variety or Musical)	**Carol Burnett** *Julie And Carol At Carnegie Hall* And *Carol And Company*
Comedy Writing	**Carl Reiner** *The Dick Van Dyke Show*

Television rights to President Kennedy's book, PROFILES IN COURAGE, are sold to Robert Saudek Associates, which makes a deal to film it as an NBC-TV series.

U.S. Health, Education and Welfare Secretary Anthony J. Celebrezze announces five grants totaling over $700,000 for educational TV broadcast stations.

CBS uses "instant replay" for the first time during the televising of the Army-Navy football game in December.

WHAT A YEAR IT WAS!

WHEN REPORTING WAS REALLY REPORTING

CBS expands its evening newscast from 15 minutes to 30 minutes anchored by **Walter Cronkite** with **Eric Sevareid** doing analysis and commentary. Not to be outdone by CBS, NBC follows by introducing the 30-minute **"Huntley-Brinkley Report."**

David Brinkley & Chet Huntley

FAMOUS BIRTHS

Edie Falco

Alex Kingston

Lisa Kudrow

Eric McCormack

Ming-Na

Conan O'Brien

John Stamos

"STROLLING" ON SATURDAYS ONLY

Dick Clark does the final weekday broadcast of *American Bandstand,* which will now be limited to Saturday afternoons.

HEY, WHAT'S UP, DOC? NOT ANOTHER COMMERCIAL

To make more room for advertisers, CBS daytime programmer **Fred Silverman** gets rid of Saturday morning reruns and puts in two solid hours of cartoons.

THANK GOODNESS! WE DON'T HAVE TO LISTEN TO ANOTHER 10 MINUTES ON BAKED BEANS

The FCC votes to adopt, as part of its rules, the National Association of Broadcasters' voluntary code restricting time limits on radio and TV commercials.

POPULAR MUSIC

Detroit's "Motown Sound" helps increase soul music record sales.

Little Stevie Wonder is the first artist to make the #1 position simultaneously on the pop singles and albums chart.

Leading gospel singer **Mahalia Jackson** expresses disapproval of Negro religious music being turned into "pop gospel."

Mahalia Jackson

Dick Clark's traveling Caravan of Stars opens in Teaneck, New Jersey, featuring among others **Bobby Vee, Brian Hyland, the Ronettes, Little Eva** and the **Dovells**.

Belgian nun **Sister Luc-Gabrielle** becomes an overnight sensation with her single "Dominique" with her album selling 750,000 copies in the first three months.

James Brown's *Live At The Apollo* album becomes the first R&B album to sell over a million copies.

TOP ALBUMS

My Son, the Celebrity
(Allan Sherman)

★

Days of Wine and Roses
(Andy Williams)

★

Little Stevie Wonder, the 12 Year Old Genius
(Stevie Wonder)

★

In the Wind
(Peter, Paul and Mary)

Capitol, Columbia, **Decca** and RCA Victor dominate recording industry sales.

NEW RECORDING ARTISTS

The Beatles
(In North America)

Lou Christie

Jackie DeShannon

Lesley Gore

Merle Haggard

Trini Lopez

Martha & The Vandellas

Wayne Newton

The O'Jays

Wilson Pickett

Lou Rawls

Otis Redding

Righteous Brothers

Barbra Streisand

Little Stevie Wonder

GOLD RECORD AWARDS

Elvis

Tony Bennett

Harry Belafonte
Tony Bennett
Dave Brubeck
Perry Como
Ray Conniff
Percy Faith
Mantovani
Mormon Tabernacle Choir
Eugene Ormandy
Peter, Paul and Mary
Elvis Presley
Andy Williams

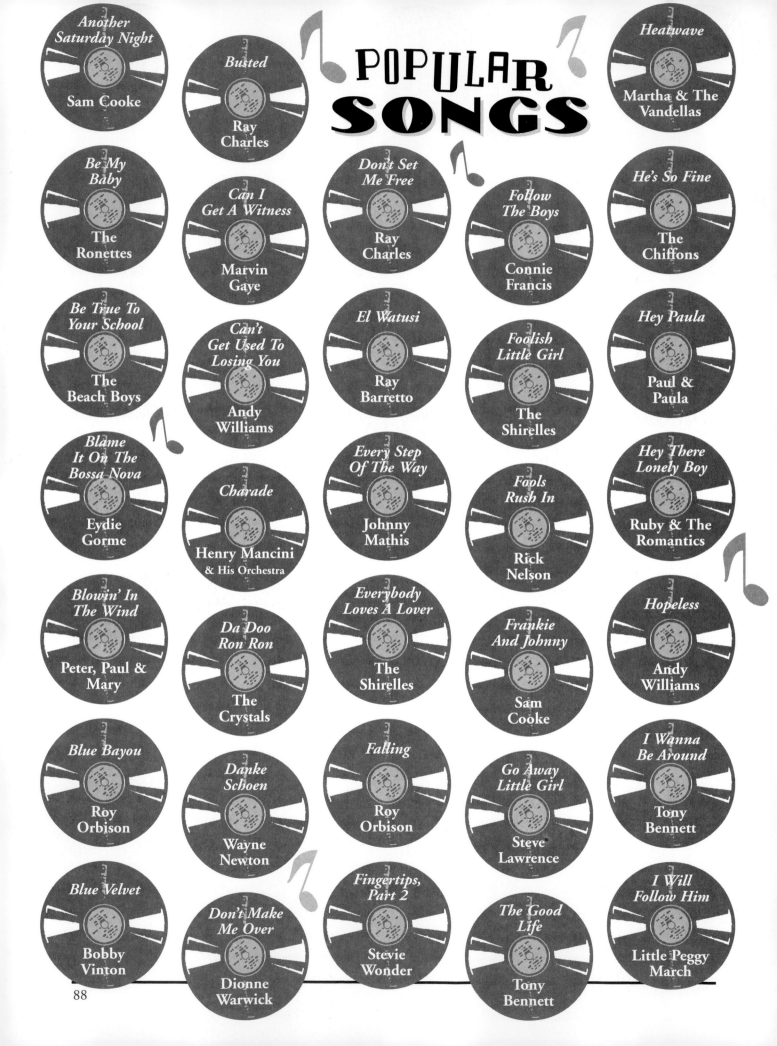

POPULAR SONGS

Another Saturday Night — Sam Cooke

Busted — Ray Charles

Heatwave — Martha & The Vandellas

Be My Baby — The Ronettes

Can I Get A Witness — Marvin Gaye

Don't Set Me Free — Ray Charles

Follow The Boys — Connie Francis

He's So Fine — The Chiffons

Be True To Your School — The Beach Boys

Can't Get Used To Losing You — Andy Williams

El Watusi — Ray Barretto

Foolish Little Girl — The Shirelles

Hey Paula — Paul & Paula

Blame It On The Bossa Nova — Eydie Gorme

Charade — Henry Mancini & His Orchestra

Every Step Of The Way — Johnny Mathis

Fools Rush In — Rick Nelson

Hey There Lonely Boy — Ruby & The Romantics

Blowin' In The Wind — Peter, Paul & Mary

Da Doo Ron Ron — The Crystals

Everybody Loves A Lover — The Shirelles

Frankie And Johnny — Sam Cooke

Hopeless — Andy Williams

Blue Bayou — Roy Orbison

Danke Schoen — Wayne Newton

Falling — Roy Orbison

Go Away Little Girl — Steve Lawrence

I Wanna Be Around — Tony Bennett

Blue Velvet — Bobby Vinton

Don't Make Me Over — Dionne Warwick

Fingertips, Part 2 — Stevie Wonder

The Good Life — Tony Bennett

I Will Follow Him — Little Peggy March

88

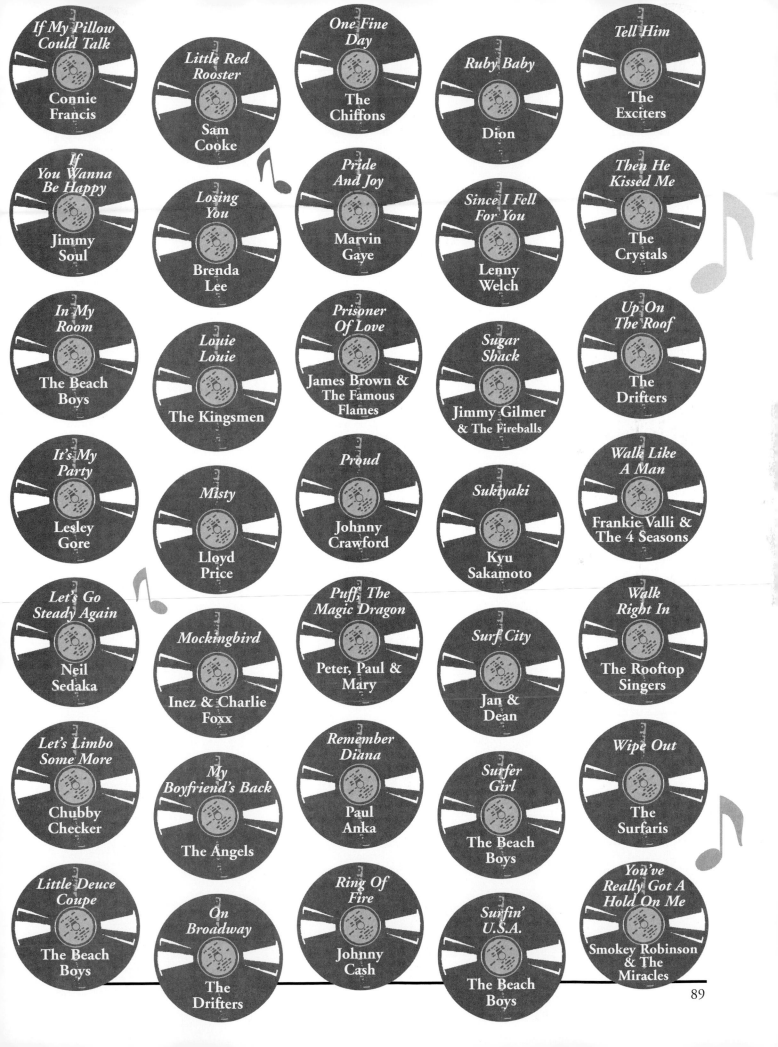

89

In a session that lasts 14 hours, the Beatles record their first British album for EMI, *Please Please Me*, with some of the cuts including "I Saw Her Standing There," "Boys," "Do You Want To Know a Secret," "There's A Place" and "Twist and Shout." In three weeks it reaches #1 on the British charts.

Vee-Jay Records, a small label out of Chicago, releases the first Beatles record, "Please Please Me" backed with "Ask Me Why." It draws very little attention despite being a smash in the U.K.

New York promoter Sid Bernstein contacts Brian Epstein, manager of the Beatles, to bring the group to the U.S., but Epstein is hesitant because the group doesn't have a hit in the States yet.

The Beatles' first U.S. album, *Introducing The Beatles*, is released by Vee-Jay Records.

NOW, WHO WAS THE GENIUS WHO TURNED THEM DOWN??

Having rejected U.S. rights to every Beatles record offered them, Capitol Records rush-releases "I Want to Hold Your Hand" backed with "I Saw Her Standing There" and within five weeks the single reaches #1 on the U.S. charts.

ROLL OVER, BEETHOVEN

The music critics of the *London Times* name John Lennon and Paul McCartney "the outstanding composers of 1963" with the Sunday *Times'* music critic Richard Buckle proclaiming them "the greatest composers since Beethoven."

The Beatles appear at the Royal Command Performances in London before a glittering audience, which includes the Queen Mother, Princess Margaret and Lord Snowden. John Lennon says, "Will people in the cheaper seats clap your hands? All the rest of you, just rattle your jewelry."

With advance orders exceeding 700,000, the Beatles' fifth British single "I Want to Hold Your Hand" is released, with the record selling one million copies, making it their second million-seller.

The Beatles' "She Loves You" hits #1 in England.

In the first outbreak of "Beatlemania," thousand of fans jam the streets and battle with police to catch a glimpse of Paul, John, Ringo and George as they arrive for an appearance on BBC's *Sunday Night at the Palladium*.

THEY'RE COMING, YEAH, YEAH, YEAH

The Beatles leave for their first tour outside of Great Britain and discover that "Beatlemania" has spread across the ocean.

Eric Clapton quits the **Roosters** to form **Casey Jones and the Engineers**.

Eric Clapton is asked to replace Anthony Topham in the **Yardbirds**.

ROCKIN' & ROLLIN' IN L.A.

L.A.'s first rock club, The Whiskey-A-Go-Go, opens its doors on Sunset Boulevard.

LET'S GET STONED

Two weeks after 19-year-old Andrew Loog Oldham signs the Rolling Stones, he produces their first recording session where they record Chuck Berry's "Come On" and Willie Dixon's "I Want to be Loved" for their first single.

The Rolling Stones make their TV debut on *Thank Your Lucky Stars* following the release of "Come On," their first record.

The Rolling Stones open their first English tour with the Everly Brothers and Bo Diddley at the New Victoria in London.

A DOZEN REASONS FOR CADILLAC'S GREATEST YEAR!

And who could help but fall in love with all of them? Each of these motor cars brings a new sense of beauty and style . . . a new dimension of performance and riding ease . . . and a new measure of comfort and luxury to motoring. And when you add the advantage of choice (143 interior selections, 106 exterior color combinations and a host of personal options) it is little wonder that 1963 is welcoming more new Cadillac owners than any previous year. Which Cadillac shall we start building for you?

Cadillac Motor Car Division • General Motors Corporation

Left, top to bottom: Coupe de Ville; Convertible; Fleetwood Sixty Special Sedan; Eldorado Biarritz; Sedan de Ville (six window); Fleetwood Seventy-Five Limousine. Right, top to bottom: Sixty-Two Sedan (four window); Sedan de Ville (four window); Sixty-Two Sedan (six window); Sixty-Two Coupe; Park Avenue Sedan de Ville; Fleetwood Seventy-Five Sedan

91

1963

Jazz King **Louis Armstrong**, *on tour in Australia, denies any plans for retirement, saying: "I'm going to go on playing till the good Lord cuts me down."*

ALL THAT JAZZ & BLUES

Vibraharpist **Lionel Hampton** packs them in on his five-week tour of Japan where Japanese jazzmen jam with him.

Lena Horne announces she will give up nightclub appearances following her stint at Manhattan's Waldorf-Astoria.

Count Basie *enjoys his greatest success in his 28 years as a bandleader with four of his albums becoming best sellers, two of which are with* Frank Sinatra *and* Ella Fitzgerald.

TOP JAZZ PERFORMERS
(Downbeat)

SOLOIST	Thelonious Monk
BANDS	Duke Ellington, Count Basie
JAZZ GROUP	Dave Brubeck
INSTRUMENTALISTS	Charlie Byrd, Ray Brown, Joe Morello, Roland Kirk, Jimmy Smith
VOCALISTS	Ella Fitzgerald, Ray Charles
VOCAL GROUP	Lambert, Hendricks and Ross

Dionne Warwick is introduced by *Marlene Dietrich* in Paris.

Doris Day, Bing Crosby, Louis Armstrong and *Nat "King" Cole* are among the singers who contribute their talents to one of the first successful charity albums – *All Star Festival* – donating their royalties to the United Nations Refugees Fund.

Frank Sinatra commemorates U.N. Staff Day with a performance at the U.N., singing these songs:

- *Too Marvelous For Words*
- *They Can't Take That Away From Me*
- *I Have Dreamed*
- *Monologue*
- *A Foggy Day*
- *My Heart Stood Still*
- *I Get A Kick Out Of You*

Record of the Year
THE DAYS OF WINE AND ROSES
Henry Mancini

Song of the Year
THE DAYS OF WINE AND ROSES
Johnny Mercer and Henry Mancini, songwriters

Album of the Year
THE BARBRA STREISAND ALBUM
Barbra Streisand

Vocal Performance, Female
THE BARBRA STREISAND ALBUM
Barbra Streisand

Vocal Performance, Male
WIVES AND LOVERS
Jack Jones

Vocal Performance, Group
BLOWIN' IN THE WIND
Peter, Paul and Mary

Folk Recording
BLOWIN' IN THE WIND
Peter, Paul and Mary

Rhythm & Blues Performance
BUSTED
Ray Charles

Instrumental Arrangement
I CAN'T STOP LOVING YOU
Quincy Jones, arranger
Count Basie, artist

Comedy Album
HELLO MUDDAH, HELLO FADDAH
Allan Sherman

THAT'S COUNTRY

Nashville surpasses Hollywood as the second largest popular music center after New York.

The Singers With The Hits

Marty Robbins
Flatt & Scruggs
Bill Anderson
Hawkshaw Hawkins
Buck Owens
Johnny Cash
George Hamilton IV
Ernest Ashworth

Patsy Cline, the 30-year-old country singer who won crossover popularity with pop Top 20 hits like "Crazy" and "I Fall to Pieces," is killed in a small plane crash near Camden, Tennessee on a flight en route to Nashville from St. Louis.

Famous BIRTHS

Sheryl Crow
M.C. Hammer
Whitney Houston
Julian Lennon
Natalie Merchant
George Michael
Anne-Sophie Mutter
Seal
Travis Tritt

Passings

Elmore James, 45
Edith Piaf, 47
Dinah Washington, 39

dylan's corner

HE'S NOT JUST BLOWIN' IN THE WIND

Billboard reviews Bob Dylan's first major solo concert at New York's Town Hall, writing that "Dylan...is the stuff of which legends are made...his talent will be around for a long, long time."

Following CBS censors forbidding him to perform his "Talking John Birch Society Blues," Bob Dylan walks out of dress rehearsals for *The Ed Sullivan Show* and refuses to appear on the show.

Bob Dylan and Joan Baez team up with Pete Seeger at the first Monterey Folk Festival.

TALK ABOUT TYPECASTING

Bob Dylan plays the part of a folk singer in the BBC radio broadcast of *The Madhouse Castle Street*.

Bob Dylan's second LP, *The Freewheelin' Bob Dylan*, the first album to feature mostly originals including "Blowin' In The Wind," hits LP chart.

A two-record "bootleg" set of Bob Dylan songs, called *The Great White Wonder*, first appears in a Los Angeles record store and is believed to be the first bootleg album.

Due to pressure from folksingers boycotting television's *Hootenanny* program, ABC invites **Pete Seeger** to appear on the show if he signs an oath of loyalty to the U.S. He refuses and ABC extends its ban on the outspoken leftist musician.

The **Weavers**, America's most popular folk group, give their farewell concert at Orchestra Hall in Chicago.

Peter, Paul and Mary, the folksinging trio who along with **Joan Baez** have introduced songwriters like **Bob Dylan** to mainstream audiences, hold top positions on the pop chart with "Blowin' In The Wind" and "Don't Think Twice, It's Alright."

With interest in folk music soaring, after a four-year hiatus the Newport Folk Festival reopens with appearances by Bob Dylan, Peter, Paul and Mary, and Joan Baez, who is queen of the festival.

Peter, Paul and Mary perform "Blowin' In The Wind" before civil rights marchers gathered in Washington.

Peter, Paul and Mary

93

Classical Music

Classical records produced 20% of record sales this year.

Itzhak Perlman makes his debut.

61-year-old **Rudolph Bing** has a new four-year contract from the Metropolitan Opera.

President Kennedy joins Rudolph Bing to announce the formation of the Metropolitan Opera National Company scheduled to go on tour in two years.

Dmitri Shostakovich has a successful premiere in Moscow's Stanislavsky Theater of the revised version of his opera *Lady Macbeth of Mtsensk*.

Celebrations mark the 150th anniversary of **Verdi** and **Wagner**.

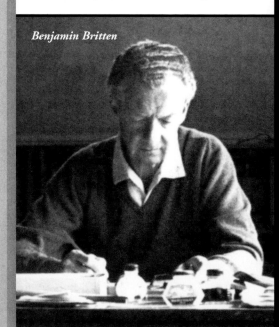

Benjamin Britten

TWO TOP CLASSICAL ALBUMS

Concert in the Park
Arthur Fiedler and the Boston Pops Orchestra

Great Scenes from Porgy and Bess
Leontyne Price and William Warfield

DEBUTS

Symphony no. 9
Roy Harris
(Pennsylvania)

•

Andromache's Farewell
Samuel Barber
(New York)

•

Concerto for Organ and Orchestra
Paul Hindemith
(New York)

•

Sept répons des ténèbres
Francis Poulenc

PULITZER PRIZE
Music

Piano Concerto no. 1
by Samuel Barber

Premiered with the Boston Symphony at Philharmonic Hall on September 24, 1962.

Opera News

Leonard Bernstein makes his debut conducting *Eugene Onegin* and **Loren Maazel** conducts *Don Giovanni*.

Leonard Bernstein

OPERA Premieres

Labyrinth
Gian Carlo Menotti
(NBC-TV)

The Death of the Bishop of Brindisi
Gian Carlo Menotti
(Ohio)

Highway No. 1, U.S.A.
William Grant Still
(Miami)

Gentlemen, Be Seated!
Jerome Moross
(New York)

The Sojourner and Mollie Sinclair
Carlisle Floyd
(North Carolina)

The Long Christmas Dinner
Paul Hindemith
(New York)

METROPOLIAN OPERA PERFORMANCES

Madama Butterfly
George Shirley

La sonnambula
Joan Sutherland

Der Rosenkavalier
Regine Crespin
Herta Topper

Otello
James McCracken

Andrea Chenier
Eileen Farrell
Franco Corelli

Gian Carlo Menotti

Dance

The Ford Foundation donates $7.7 million to the development of ballet in the U.S. to the following companies:

Manhattan's School of American Ballet
N.Y. City Ballet
School of American Ballet (N.Y.)
San Francisco Ballet
National Ballet Co. (Washington)
Pennsylvania Ballet Co.
Utah Ballet Co.
Houston Ballet Co.
Boston Ballet Co.

Martha Graham *and her dance company perform at the Edinburgh Festival and in London.*

NEW WORKS

Movements for Piano and Orchestra
George Balanchine

•

Scudorama
Paul Taylor

•

Imago
Alwin Nikolais

William Christensen forms **Ballet West** in Salt Lake City.

•

The **Pennsylvania Ballet** is created.

•

The Cultural Presentations Program of the U.S. Department of State sponsors a tour of the Middle and Far East of the **Robert Joffrey Ballet**.

•

The **New York City Ballet** premieres *Movements For Piano And Orchestra* with music by **Stravinsky** and choreography by **George Balanchine**.

•

The **Royal Ballet**, featuring prima ballerina **Margot Fonteyn** and ex-Soviet dancer **Rudolf Nureyev**, perform at New York's Metropolitan Opera House.

•

After a little under a year in Washington, D.C., the **American Ballet Theatre** returns to New York.

•

The newly formed company, **National Ballet**, gives its first performance in Washington, D.C.

•

Following being made a Dame Commander of the Order of the British Empire in **Queen Elizabeth's** Birthday Honors List, British prima ballerina **Alicia Markova** takes over as director of the **Metropolitan Opera Ballet** in New York.

•

The **31st Jacob's Pillow Dance Festival** held at Lee, Massachusetts is well attended.

ON BROADWAY

With Laurence Olivier at its head, Britain's National Theatre presents its first production, HAMLET, starring Peter O'Toole, Rosemary Harris and Michael Redgrave.

Laurence Olivier

Barbra Streisand steals the show in the Broadway musical I CAN GET IT FOR YOU WHOLESALE.

Liza Minnelli makes a breakthrough in her career in BEST FOOT FORWARD.

Barbra Streisand

Liza Minnelli

1963

ANOTHER OPENING, ANOTHER NIGHT

Barbara Cook and
Daniel Massey
in *She Loves Me*

BAREFOOT IN THE PARK
Robert Redford

Elizabeth Ashley

ENTER LAUGHING
Vivian Blaine   Alan Arkin

Sylvia Sidney

A CASE OF LIBEL
Sidney Blackmer   Van Heflin

NOBODY LOVES AN ALBATROSS
Robert Preston

LUTHER
Albert Finney

THE BALLAD OF THE SAD CAFÉ
Colleen Dewhurst

Michael Dunn

MOTHER COURAGE AND HER CHILDREN
Anne Bancroft

THE MILK TRAIN DOESN'T STOP HERE ANYMORE
Mildred Dunnock

OLIVER!
Clive Revill   Bruce Prochnik

Georgia Brown

110 IN THE SHADE
Robert Horton   Inga Swenson

THE PRIVATE EAR, THE PUBLIC EYE
Barry Foster

ONE FLEW OVER THE CUCKOO'S NEST
Gene Wilder   Kirk Douglas

THE REHEARSAL
Keith Michell   Alan Badel

SHE LOVES ME
Jack Cassidy   Barbara Cook

TOVARICH
Vivien Leigh

Jean-Pierre Aumont

Classics & Revivals

Cyril Ritchard, David Wayne and **Glynis Johns** in *Too True To Be Good*

The Maids
Jean Genet

In White America
Martin B. Duberman

The Bald Soprano
Eugene Ionesco

The Lesson
Eugene Ionesco

The Trojan Women
Euripides

Too True To Be Good
George Bernard Shaw

The School For Scandal
Richard Brinsley Sheridan

Desire Under The Elms
Eugene O'Neill

Strange Interlude
Eugene O'Neill

A Month In The Country
Ivan Turgenev

WHAT ELSE IS RUNNING

A Rainy Day In Newark

✣

The Advocate

✣

Ages Of Man

✣

Andorra

✣

The Beast In Me

✣

Bicycle Ride To Nevada

✣

Brigadoon

✣

Children From Their Games

✣

Chips With Everything

✣

Dear Me, The Sky Is Falling

The Vivian Beaumont is the first New York theater to install an electronically controlled lighting system.

The Minnesota Theatre Company is founded by Sir Tyrone Guthrie and kicks off its first repertory season with *Hamlet, The Miser, Death Of A Salesman* and *The Three Sisters*.

Arthur Miller meets with his cast and director **Elia Kazan** for a reading of his new play, *After The Fall*.

Teenagers perform *Babes In Arms* as their summer project at the Henry Street Settlement in New York City.

In order to encourage amateur theater to produce new plays, 10 famous American playwrights, members of the American Playwrights Theater, including **Robert Anderson, William Saroyan** and **S. N. Behrman**, write new plays for the exclusive use of at least 50 amateur theaters for a period of one year.

New York State's attorney general's office holds a two-day public hearing on the results of an eight-month investigation into the irregularities of theater financing including scalper ticket pricing.

The Golden Age

✣

Here's Love

✣

The Heroine

✣

The Hollow Crown

✣

Hot Spot

✣

The Irregular Verb To Love

✣

Jennie

✣

The King And I

✣

The Lady Of The Camellias

✣

Lorenzo

✣

Man And Boy

✣

My Mother, My Father And Me

✣

Natural Affection

In the air and over there, enjoy the Priceless Extra of Experience!

Wherever in the world you travel you're better off with Pan Am —world's most experienced airline!

(See your Pan Am Travel Agent)

FIRST ON THE ATLANTIC
FIRST ON THE PACIFIC
FIRST IN LATIN AMERICA
FIRST 'ROUND THE WORLD

Only Pan Am offers you Jets from the U.S. direct to a grand total of 22 European cities, including London, Paris and Rome

WHAT ELSE IS RUNNING

Oh Dad, Poor Dad, Mama's Hung You In The Closet And I'm Feelin' So Sad

✿

Oklahoma!

✿

On An Open Roof

✿

Once For The Asking

✿

Pajama Tops

✿

Pal Joey

✿

Photo Finish

✿

Rattle Of A Simple Man

✿

The Resistible Rise Of Arturo Ui

THE FINAL CURTAIN

The Sound of Music

Mary Martin
Theodore Bikel

•

Camelot

Julie Andrews
Richard Burton

•

Carnival!

Anna Maria Alberghetti
Jerry Orbach

The Riot Act

✿

Semi-Detached

✿

Sophie

✿

Spoon River Anthology

✿

The Student Gypsy

✿

Tambourines To Glory

Geraldine McEwan and **John Gielgud** in *The School For Scandal* (revival)

WHAT A YEAR IT WAS!

TONY AWARDS
1963

PLAY
"Who's Afraid Of Virginia Woolf?"

•

MUSICAL PLAY
"A Funny Thing Happened On The Way To The Forum"

•

DRAMATIC ACTOR
Arthur Hill
"Who's Afraid Of Virginia Woolf?"

•

DRAMATIC ACTRESS
Uta Hagen
"Who's Afraid Of Virginia Woolf?"

MUSICAL ACTOR
Zero Mostel
"A Funny Thing Happened On The Way To The Forum"

•

MUSICAL ACTRESS
Vivien Leigh
"Tovarich"

•

CHOREOGRAPHY
Bob Fosse
"Little Me"

NEW YORK DRAMA CRITICS' CIRCLE AWARDS

BEST PLAY	**WHO'S AFRAID OF VIRGINIA WOOLF?** Edward Albee (playwright)
SPECIAL CITATION	**BEYOND THE FRINGE** Alan Bennett Peter Cook Jonathan Miller and Dudley Moore

SPECIAL AWARDS

IRVING BERLIN

ALAN BENNETT, PETER COOK, JONATHAN MILLER and DUDLEY MOORE for "BEYOND THE FRINGE"

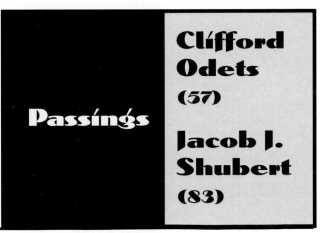

Passings

Clifford Odets (57)

Jacob J. Shubert (83)

18TH CENTURY CHIPPENDALE

19TH CENTURY DUNCAN PHYFE

20TH CENTURY NICKEL-CHROME PLATING

©1963, Inco.

The new quality look in living rooms is here: Furniture made with Nickel Plating

A new and very distinctive kind of furniture is taking its place with the quality pieces of the past. It's lustrous Nickel-Chrome Plated furniture, and it's giving today's modern homes a strikingly beautiful look.

Nickel-Chrome Plating is lighting things up. It's picking up colors (bold, dramatic colors from walls, carpets and fabrics) and bouncing them around. It's setting an elegant new style in contemporary home decor.

Nickel-Chrome Plating is also going to last. With quality Nickel Plating under chrome, this furniture has exceptional durability. Scuffs, scratches, kicks, bumps, bangs, a whole house full of kids won't spoil its good looks.

Here, as in hundreds of products — automotive brightwork, appliances, household fixtures, sporting goods, bicycles, industrial equipment, and many, many others — Nickel's contribution is quality. For additional information on this versatile, Nickel-quality finish, just write Dept. K-14,

THE INTERNATIONAL NICKEL COMPANY, INC., New York 5, New York

104

NICKEL...its contribution is **QUALITY**

ANDY WARHOL

ART

LOS ANGELES

EDWARD RUSCHA and **ROY LICHTENSTEIN** at Ferus Gallery. **FRANZ KLINE** and **ED KIENHOLZ** at Dwan Gallery.

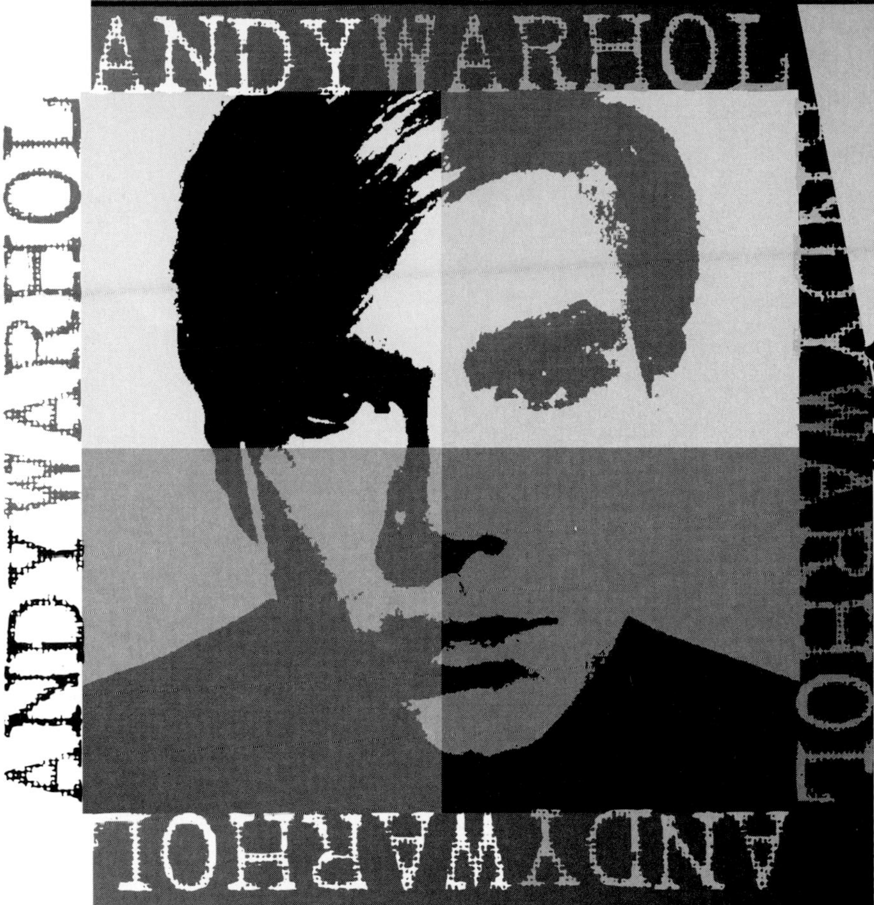

Andy has a show at the Ferus Gallery in Los Angeles. Canvases are silk-screened with pictures of Elvis Presley and Elizabeth Taylor.
--
Andy gives a party on the Santa Monica Pier.
--
Dennis Hopper takes photos of Andy. One picture ends up on the cover of "Artforum."
--
Andy begins the Factory.

The Pasadena Art Museum has its first MARCEL DUCHAMP retrospective. The museum also holds a WASSILY KANDINSKY show emphasizing works from the '20s, '30s and '40s. A larger Kandinsky retrospective is seen at Manhattan's Guggenheim Museum.

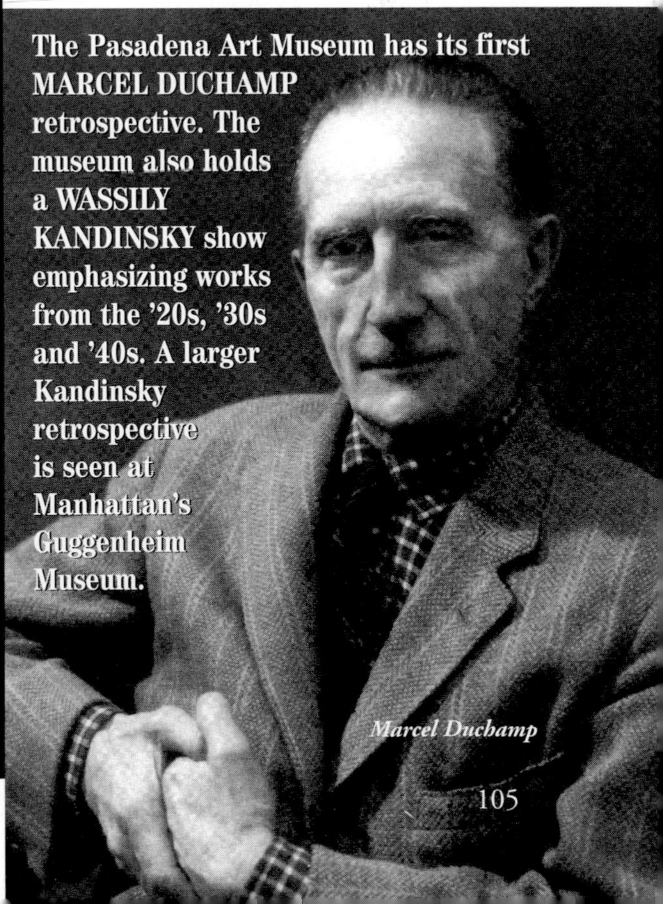

Marcel Duchamp

WHAT A YEAR IT WAS!

1963

Hans Hofmann, Alexander Calder and **Ad Reinhardt** are winners at the Art Institute of Chicago's 66th Annual of American Painting and Sculpture.

Oskar Kokoschka and **Alberto Giacometti** are elected honorary members of the American Academy and National Institute of Arts.

The British Order of Merit is bestowed on **Henry Moore**.

Kokoschka drawing

Andrew Wyeth is awarded the Presidential Medal of Freedom.

Louise Nevelson becomes president of Artists Equity Association.

The first large showing of pop art, "Six Painters and the Object," is seen at the Guggenheim Museum and the Los Angeles County Museum. Featured artists include **Warhol, Rauschenberg, Johns, Dine** and **Lichtenstein.**

The Philadelphia Museum show, "Philadelphia Collects 20th Century," features mostly works from private collections by **Rothko, Dine, Oldenburg, Rauschenberg, de Kooning, Braque, Picasso, Pollock, Matisse** and **Kandinsky.**

new york shows

if i can make it there, i can make it anywhere...

Robert Rauschenberg	Jewish Museum
Francis Bacon	Guggenheim Museum
Auguste Rodin	Museum of Modern Art
Hans Hofmann	Museum of Modern Art
Joan Miro	Pierre Matisse Gallery
Alexander Calder	Perls Gallery
Paul Klee	New Arts Center
Isamu Noguchi	Cordier & Ekstrom
Edward Kienholz	Iolas Gallery
Jim Dine	Sidney Janis Gallery

Manhattan's Asia House features Buddha, with statues and paintings from India, Nepal, China, Cambodia, Thailand and other Asian nations.

WHAT A YEAR IT WAS!

THE LATEST

Claes Oldenburg	*Soft Pay-Telephone*
Robert Rauschenberg	*Barge*
Andy Warhol	*Orange Disaster #5*
Roy Lichtenstein	*Wham!*
Larry Rivers	*Dutch Masters*
Helen Frankenthaler	*Blue Atmosphere*
Ellsworth Kelly	*Red Blue Green*
Jasper Johns	*Map*
George Segal	*Cinema*
Elaine de Kooning	*Robert Mallary, Version 2*
Jim Dine	*5 Palettes*

AUCTION HIGHLIGHTS

Degas	*Green Dancer*	$294,000
Rembrandt	*Portrait of a Young Girl*	$260,000
Monet	*Waterlilies*	$137,500
Gauguin	*The Washerwoman*	$110,000
Picasso	*Seated Nude*	$57,500
Chagall	*Notre Dame*	$43,000
de Kooning	*Two Standing Women*	$27,000

(auction record for de Kooning)

Goya's painting "The Bookseller" is bequeathed to Washington's National Gallery while New York Governor **Nelson Rockefeller** gives **Matisse's** "The Dance" to the Museum of Modern Art.

Paintings by **Monet, Morisot, Bonnard, Manet, Corot** and others are donated to the National Museum of Wales.

Elizabeth Taylor purchases **Van Gogh's** "View of the St. Remy Hospital" for $257,600.

Passings

William Baziotes (50)
Georges Braque (81)
Jacques Villon
(Gaston Duchamp) (87)

WHAT A YEAR IT WAS!

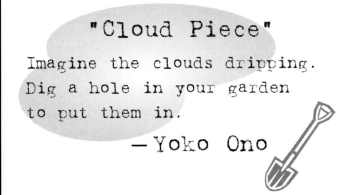

"Cloud Piece"

Imagine the clouds dripping.
Dig a hole in your garden
to put them in.

— Yoko Ono

1963

MAN RAY'S autobiography, "Self Portrait," is published.

LeRoy Neiman is a new name in the painting world, with his bright, vivid images of sports-related themes.

She's So Lovely

On loan from the Louvre in Paris, Leonardo da Vinci's "Mona Lisa" is on display at Washington's National Gallery where a half million people view her. President Kennedy attends the opening festivities. The painting is later moved to the Metropolitan Museum of Art in New York.

EUROPEAN TIDBITS

A WOODEN CRUCIFIX BELIEVED TO HAVE BEEN CARVED BY A TEENAGE **MICHELANGELO** IS FOUND IN A FLORENCE MONASTERY.

LE CORBUSIER IS CHOSEN TO BUILD FRANCE'S MUSEUM OF MODERN ART.

HENRY MOORE SCULPTURES ARE SEEN AT MARLBOROUGH NEW LONDON GALLERY IN LONDON.

THE **PICASSO** MUSEUM IN BARCELONA OPENS.

To help foster your child's creativity and imagination, Kathryn Delphrey, an Albuquerque, New Mexico art consultant, suggests skipping the coloring books and offering instead blank paper and paints or crayons.

I NEED PANTS, A LAWN MOWER AND, OH YES, A PAINTING FOR THE LIVING ROOM

Though an unlikely place to purchase fine art, **Sears, Roebuck & Co.** sells thousands of original paintings.

WHAT A YEAR IT WAS!

Books

 **1963**

Nobel Prize for Literature
GIORGOS SEFERIS, Greece

Pulitzer Prizes

FICTION
The Reivers — WILLIAM FAULKNER

HISTORY
Washington, Village And Capital, 1800-1878 — CONSTANCE McLAUGHLIN GREEN

BIOGRAPHY OR AUTOBIOGRAPHY
Henry James — LEON EDEL

POETRY
Pictures From Breughel — WILLIAM CARLOS WILLIAMS

GENERAL NON-FICTION
The Guns Of August — BARBARA W. TUCHMAN

American Academy of Arts & Letters

GOLD MEDAL FOR POETRY
WILLIAM CARLOS WILLIAMS (posthumously)

Bollingen Poetry Prize
ROBERT FROST

National Book Award
Morte d'Urban J. F. POWERS

The American Library Association gives the John Newbery Medal for the "most distinguished contribution to American literature for children" to Madeleine L'Engle for *A Wrinkle In Time*.

THERE'S NO ACCOUNTING FOR TASTE

While the New Orleans Police Department arrests and attempts to prosecute a bookseller on obscenity charges for selling James Baldwin's *Another Country*, district attorney Jim Garrison criticizes censorship and does not prosecute.

The New York State Court of Appeals rules that Henry Miller's *Tropic of Cancer* is "dirt for dirt's sake" and is "flagrantly obscene."

Sir Winston Churchill bestows the colossal task of writing his biography to his journalist son, Randolph.

For raising the nation's awareness to the dangers of pesticides in her book, **Silent Spring**, Rachel Carson receives the Audubon Medal of the National Audubon Society, the first woman awarded the honor.

Sylvia Plath uses the pseudonym Victoria Lucas for her book, *The Bell Jar*.

PASSINGS

Jean Cocteau (74)
Robert Frost (88)
Aldous Huxley (69)
C. S. Lewis (64)
Sylvia Plath (30)
William Carlos Williams (79)

 **WHAT A YEAR IT WAS!**

Books

Leonard Cohen

James Baldwin

A Kind Of Magic
Edna Ferber

•

**A Man And
Two Women**
Doris Lessing

•

A Sense Of Reality
Graham Greene

•

**The American
Way Of Death**
Jessica Mitford

•

Approach To Vedanta
Christopher Isherwood

•

The Bell Jar
Sylvia Plath

•

The Benefactor
Susan Sontag

•

Boulder Dam
Zane Grey

•

Caravans
James A. Michener

Cat's Cradle
Kurt Vonnegut

•

The Centaur
John Updike

•

City Of Night
John Rechy

•

**The Cold War
And
The Income Tax**
Edmund Wilson

•

Dr. Seuss's ABC
Theodor "Dr. Seuss"
Geisel

•

Ehrengard
Isak Dinesen

•

**Eichmann In
Jerusalem: A
Report On The
Banality Of Evil**
Hannah Arendt

•

**The Favorite
Game**
Leonard Cohen

•

**The Feminine
Mystique**
Betty Friedan

Fifty Poems
Boris Pasternak

•

The Fire Next Time
James Baldwin

•

The Glass Blowers
Daphne Du Maurier

•

The Group
Mary McCarthy

•

**Happiness Is A
Warm Puppy**
Charles M. Schulz

•

The Hat On The Bed
John O'Hara

•

I Owe Russia $1,200
Bob Hope

•

Idiots First
Bernard Malamud

•

**Israel: Years
Of Challenge**
David Ben-Gurion

V. S. Naipaul

Jacques Cousteau

WHAT A YEAR IT WAS!

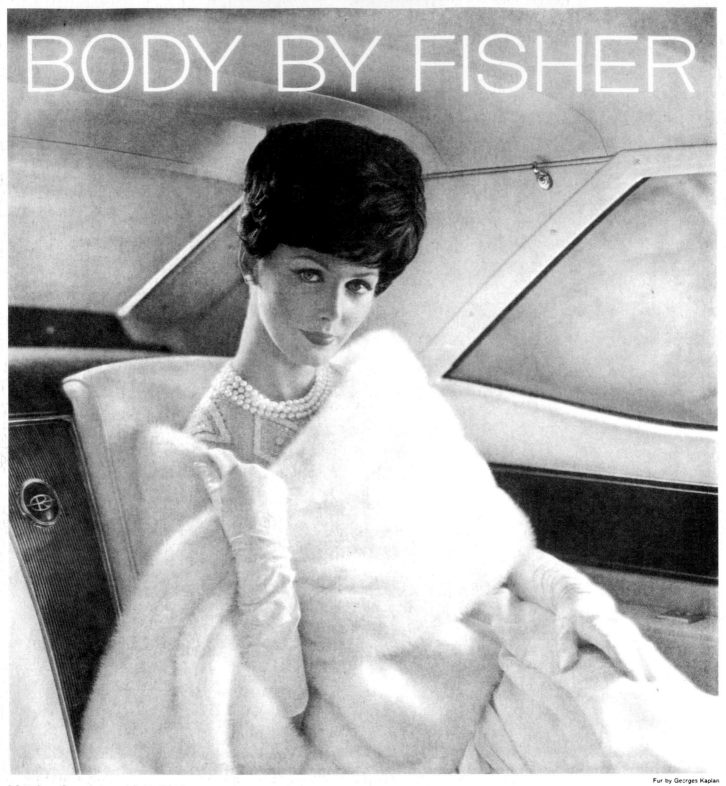

BODY BY FISHER

Fur by Georges Kaplan

You're fresher with Fisher

You get a car-full of clean, fresh air twice a minute—even with the windows shut! You feel as refreshed as if you were riding on a cloud. Our Snorkel System does it. And it comes only with Body by Fisher—the most carefully crafted, solidly built, longest lasting car body ever. So much of the buy is in the body. And Body by Fisher makes a GM car a <u>better</u> buy: Chevrolet, Pontiac, Oldsmobile, Buick, Cadillac.

Body by Fisher

GENERAL MOTORS SYMBOL OF QUALITY

112

Fashion TRENDS

Pink and white, alone or together, are the year's must-have colors.

Hemlines hover at or just north of the knee.

Sleeveless dresses for the young and the young at heart.

Long dresses for evening outings and parties are a fashionable look.

Brocade theater suits for a show, dinner or a grand night out on the town.

Sportswear and relaxed clothing gain acceptance everywhere.

Waist-less "shift" dresses are all the rage.

WHAT A YEAR IT WAS!

PARIS!

DIOR

Linen, flowers, pink, Chantilly lace, long dresses, mid-length dresses, low décolletage, ruffles, satin, sashes, overblouses, boleros, short skirts, low backs, Breton hats, short jackets, low necklines, gloves.

GIVENCHY

Belts, loose jackets, beige, black, blue, linen, sleeveless dresses, mother of pearl, tulle, embroidery, sequins, satin, bathing suits.

ST. LAURENT

White piqué, high seams, navy, turtleneck dresses, crepe, cardigans, short skirts, topcoats, boots, suede, funnel necks, satin, sleeveless, embroidery, small buttons, tweed coats, jersey dresses, shirt-jackets, ruffles, sashes.

CHANEL

White, worsted, pearls, rubies, sapphires, pleats, black & white, gilt buttons, cravats, lawn shirts, silk sweaters, navy blazers, gold brocade, cardigan jackets.

BALENCIAGA

Yellow, scarlet, violet, taupe, capes, pearls, silk, stoles, taffeta, floor-length coats, raincoats, belts, oversized buttons, bejeweled evening bags.

WHAT A YEAR IT WAS!

1963

Italian Fashion

MAINBOCHER
Chiffon, organdy, crepe, sleeveless blouses, organza, brocade, taffeta, ankle-length dresses, wool suits, tweed, beige, gabardine, piqué, navy.

COURRÈGES
Boots, gloves, slim slacks, narrow coats, brown, wool, domed hats, white, camel hair, checks, tweed, green, silk, evening pajamas.

Emilio Pucci presents brilliantly colored casual wear and bathing suits including a Japanese-style kimono and a one-piece silk dress of green, magenta and chartreuse.

A Liberal Party candidate for Italy's Chamber of Deputies, **Pucci** creates scarves decorated with the slogan "Vote Liberal."

Roberto Cappucci
has his first Paris fashion show.

Gucci stores open in Paris, London and Palm Beach.

WHAT A YEAR IT WAS!

1963
PARIS DESIGNERS UNVEIL

With Easter not far away, Paris designers stage a preview of their spring hats.

Paris seems to be encouraging the return of the wide-brim hats that flirt with that come-hither look.

Their Spring Hats

You can have ornate or severe. But, all in all, simplicity seems to be the keynote — the kind of simplicity that makes a bonnet exclusive and expensive.

Hat designers can really run wild and usually do. This collection offers something for every taste but not necessarily every pocketbook. See you in the Easter Parade!

There are two ways to a woman's heart. One is FAME de CORDAY

No other gift delights so instantly, then lingers so memorably. Pictured here, from the exquisite FAME Christmas collection: FAME Purse Perfume Spray, 5.00. Deluxe Spraygrance Cologne, 5.00. FAME Perfume, 6.50 to 35.00.

Fine perfumes imported from France, other products blended in U.S.A. with domestic and imported essences.   ©1963 PARFUMS CORDAY, INC.

And Now, A Fashion Word From LONDON

1963

Spring hats are coming up roses and every other flower. These London fashions are like a breath of May to anyone who has been shut up all winter.

Mod British designer **Mary Quant** introduces her line of mass-marketed fashions called the Ginger Group.

•

Vidal Sassoon creates the bob, a short, pointed haircut.

Princess Margaret's designer, Simon Berman, presents this organdy confection.

This creation, inspired by the days of King Edward VII, has a personality all its own.

Spats have been taken over by the fair sex and go with fashionable jewelry in matched sets of bracelet, belt and necklace.

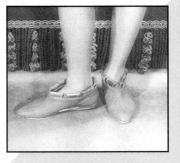

Booties are finding a place for casual wear. Featured are soft leather trimmed with gold and a storm boot trimmed with rhinestones.

1963

Boots

are de rigueur, be they ankle, mid-calf or all the way up to the thigh.

Flat, comfortable, multi-hued shoes made of linen can fill all your daytime feet needs and are the "in" look. Oxfords, sneakers and T-strap sandals are other casual choices.

A London company introduces a women's shoe with a tiny wheel on the heel. The wheel is supposed to make walking more comfortable, increase the life of the heel and protect carpets and wooden floors from sharp heels.

for the feet

WHAT A YEAR IT WAS!

Sailing pants, parka, White Stag

Pink checked slacks, Jax

<u>With Tampax, you sail through life</u>. Nothing hampers you, nothing hinders you. Tampax is invisible, unfelt in place . . . wonderful!

<u>With Tampax, you're always at ease</u>. Nothing can show, no one can know. Slender fashions become you. You feel confidence, security!

You feel so cool, so clean, so fresh with **TAMPAX** Worn internally, it's the modern way

121

1963

The Finishing Touches

Bracelets, necklaces, earrings, rings and pins are large with lots of gold, rhinestones and a variety of real and faux stones.

Handbags are large while buttons for jackets are crafted with real stones.

MAKEUP

Estée Lauder

presents the Castilian Look — a dazzling mouth, gray eye shadow, lustrous foundation and a coral-tinted rouge.

Eyes are big,

with thick eyelashes, lots of liner and shadow, topped by thick, well-arched brows.

Max Factor brings out textured Lash Full for thicker, longer and darker lashes.

Lips are **full**

and quite kissable thanks to Germaine Monteil's new colors — Burgundy Red, Claret Red, Cherry Brandy and Rose, all topped by the shimmering Lumium Plus.

WHAT A YEAR IT WAS!

FASHION NEWS
FROM MONACO

Ford's lively new look makes headlines!

Right in the middle of the automotive year...right in sports car-loving Monaco . . . Ford introduced the liveliest of the lively ones.

63½ Super Torque Ford Sports Hardtop At the left, in front of the Monte Carlo Casino, stands newsmaker number one. It's the hardtop that looks like a convertible... the sleek Super Torque Ford Sports Hardtop! Choose the XL model and relax in deep-foam bucket seats... with console-mounted shift at your fingertips. There's also a bench seat model . . . and your choice of Thunderbird V-8s up to 425 hp.

63½ Falcon Hardtop On the right is the luxurious new Falcon Hardtop. Its racy new roofline adds a new fashion flair to America's all-time Economy Champ. Available with bench seats—or in bucket seat models with console,and optional 4-speed floor shift.

Ford's lively new look will be making friends everywhere . . . on Main Street as well as in Monaco. At your Ford Dealer's now.

America's liveliest,
most care-free cars

FORD

FALCON · FAIRLANE · FORD · THUNDERBIRD

FOR 60 YEARS THE SYMBOL
OF DEPENDABLE PRODUCTS

MOTOR COMPANY

125

1963

Levi Strauss & Co.
launches a new product – preshrunk Levi's jeans.

Comfortable, colorful drawstring "Jams" shorts hit the beach.

Forget the high-cost Burberry raincoat. New York's Instant-Fold Products offers an inexpensive plastic raincoat that comes with its own carrying case.

*Visiting the folks back home, **Princess Grace** is honored by the Fashion Group of Philadelphia, benefactors of the Crystal Ball, at which she appears wearing a Balenciaga gown.*

HIP-HUGGER and BELL-BOTTOM JEANS are hip, and increasingly popular, choices for today's pants-wearing women.

At $200 an hour, beautiful **Suzy Parker** is the highest-paid model in the fashion world.

126

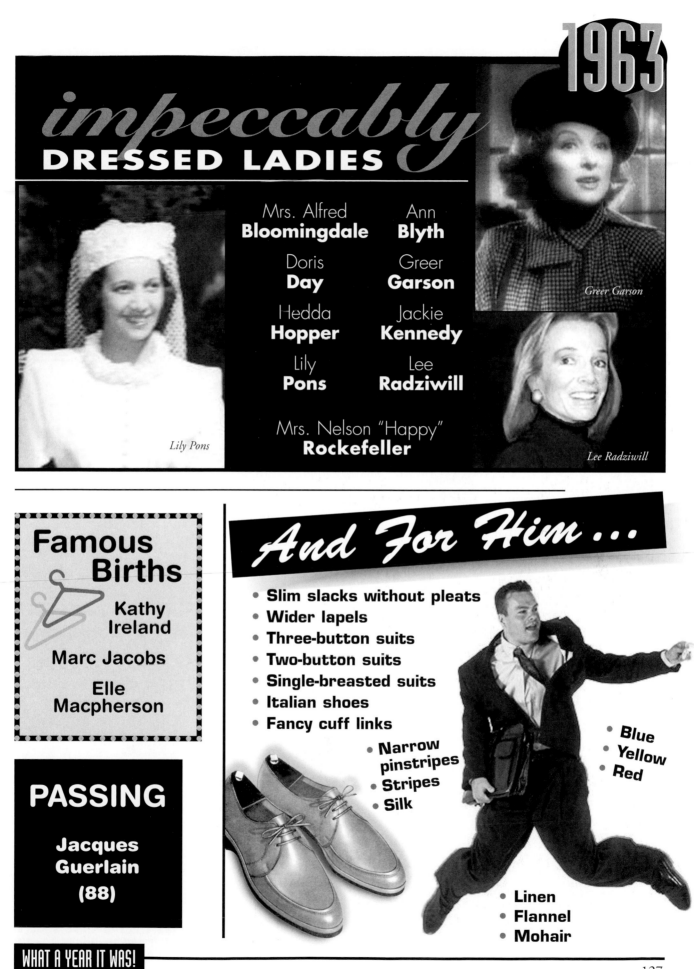

impeccably DRESSED LADIES

Mrs. Alfred **Bloomingdale**

Ann **Blyth**

Doris **Day**

Greer **Garson**

Hedda **Hopper**

Jackie **Kennedy**

Lily **Pons**

Lee **Radziwill**

Mrs. Nelson "Happy" **Rockefeller**

Greer Garson

Lee Radziwill

Lily Pons

Famous Births

Kathy Ireland

Marc Jacobs

Elle Macpherson

PASSING

Jacques Guerlain (88)

And For Him...

- Slim slacks without pleats
- Wider lapels
- Three-button suits
- Two-button suits
- Single-breasted suits
- Italian shoes
- Fancy cuff links

- Narrow pinstripes
- Stripes
- Silk

- Blue
- Yellow
- Red

- Linen
- Flannel
- Mohair

WHAT A YEAR IT WAS!

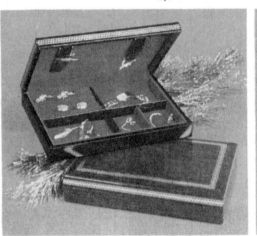

New PRODUCTS & INVENTIONS

NOW, WHAT THE HECK DID I SAY THAT COMBINATION IS?

The Thomas Edlyn Company in Collingdale, Pennsylvania is marketing a new push-button lock with over 1,000 combinations.

Mattel introduces Midge, Barbie's best girlfriend.

THIS IS ONE FOR THE BOIDS

Bird-watchers can now peek inside a nest without being seen by the birds with a new plastic wren house that attaches to a window, developed by Vu-a-Nest, Granite City, Illinois.

A patent for tab-opening aluminum cans is awarded to Ermal C. Fraze, who grants exclusive rights to Alcoa, which goes into production with 40 can manufacturers.

Successfully shedding 72 pounds, Jean Nidetch helps launch *Weight Watchers.*

Mary Kay Ash opens a small retail shop in Dallas, launching *Mary Kay Cosmetics.*

WHAT A YEAR IT WAS!

1963

she's chiquita banana and she's feeling blue

"Miss" Chiquita banana is decorated with a blue sticker for the first time.

Frozen vegetables packed in a bag that goes directly into the pot for boiling are introduced by **GREEN GIANT.**

Coca-Cola introduces **TAB**, a soft drink sweetened with cyclamates.

HERE COMES THAT SUGAR HIGH

Chips Ahoy! cookies and **Fruit Loops** hit the consumer market for the first time.

CHOCOLATE – IN THE SURVIVAL FOOD GROUP

Chuck Wagon Foods of Newton, Massachusetts has just come out with a pocket-sized emergency waterproof food kit which contains, among other survival items, a compressed cereal bar, a starch jelly bar, a tropical chocolate bar, a single-edge razor blade and fishhooks.

And now for that wonderful chemical high, try some *Cremora* non-dairy creamer in your coffee.

IS THAT A GOLF BALL IN MY ICED TEA?

Bad day on the links? Try these new 19th Hole "Golf Ball" ice cubes made with the new **Ice Ball Tray** from Marvic Corp. in Brooklyn, N.Y.

GET READY TO PARTY!

Acme-National Refrigeration of Astoria, N.Y. has introduced an ice-cube maker that can produce 40 lbs. of ice cubes a day.

CUP OF COFFEE IN 20 SECONDS

"Inventor of the Month" Luther G. Simjian, president of Reflectone Electronics, Inc., receives a patent on his cup "that orders its own coffee" through the use of a "designator" at the bottom of the cup, which for 10¢ allows you to fill 'er up at your favorite vending machine. Mr. Simjian also invented the "Bankograph," Universal's automatic bank depositing machine currently undergoing trials in New York and other cities.

GREASE NO MORE

General Electric introduces an automatic self-cleaning oven designed to save housewives from one of the dirtiest jobs in the kitchen.

Available in several finishes, including American walnut and English brown oak, the new **Avanti** refrigerator is designed to look more like a piece of furniture than a standard appliance.

WHAT A YEAR IT WAS!

HELP FOR THE HANDICAPPED

Bell Telephone introduces new devices that control the volume for the hard of hearing, an amplifier for people who can only talk in a whisper and an electronic larynx for persons without a voice box.

Commercial service of push-button telephones begins.

THERE'S A CREDIT CARD PHONE IN YOUR FUTURE

Although there are no plans at the present time to go into production, a Bell Laboratories engineer invents a credit card telephone, which the company sees as having future possibilities.

PLEASE LEAVE A MESSAGE AND WE'LL GET BACK TO YOU

New York company Mind-A-Fone is offering a compact transistorized unit called the "AnsaFone," which answers your phone in your own voice and records the caller's message automatically.

COULD YOU SPEAK INTO MY ATTACHÉ CASE, PLEASE

American Geloso Electronics in New York is offering a way to record conversations in secret with their new attaché case containing a concealed microphone capable of recording sound up to 25 feet away.

Smile, You're On Camera

Kodak's new *"Instamatic"* cameras come pre-loaded with the first film cartridges.

Polaroid introduces its entirely new, easy-to-operate *Automatic 100 Land Camera* that uses quick-loading 8-exposure film packs.

INSTANT REPLAY IN THE MAKING

For closed-circuit television recordings that can be used in education, industry, training, medical science, etc., Ampex comes out with a videotape recorder than can tape television programs or live action for playback at another time.

The *Oklahoma City Times* and the *Daily Oklahoman* are the first U.S. dailies written and typeset entirely by computer.

- - - - - -

Arthur North invents a system of teaching computers to capitalize and punctuate, enabling them to produce a more attractive typeface.

1963

DRYING BABY'S BOTTOM

A new product called "BOBABY" is designed to keep the infant dry by placing a cloth between the skin and the diaper, permitting urine to pass through to the diaper without remaining wet itself.

- - - - -

U.S. Sonics Corp. of Cambridge, Massachusetts is marketing "AQUALARM," a swimming pool alarm that sends a signal when a child or animal has fallen into the water.

- - - - -

The new collapsible "PLAYTEX BABY NURSER" claims to reduce substantially the incidence of colic by closely reproducing natural feeding action.

NOT TOO BIG, NOT TOO SMALL, BUT JUST RIGHT

"Pic-A-Size" adjustable aluminum baking pans allow housewives to choose from 40 different sizes when baking a cake.

THE CLEANERS MAKE HOUSE CALLS

Robot Industries in Bucks County, Pennsylvania is offering a mobile dry-cleaning unit called "Mister Dry Kleen."

WATCH YOUR FINGERS

St. Regis Paper of Chicago, Illinois introduces a notebook "College Binder," a three-ring loose-leaf filler pad.

DOWN UNDER

Buckminster Fuller, known for his geodesic domes, gets a patent on an underwater submarine base.

FIRST YOU SEE IT, THEN YOU DON'T

"Dissolvo" is a new water-soluble paper that dissolves in water within seconds.

SLIP & SLIDE NO MORE

"Endslip" is a new spray-on product for the bathtub which makes the tub slip-proof in less than one minute.

THE BATH BUBBLES BUBBLETH OVER

A new portable unit that converts a bathtub into a hydro-massage is introduced by the National Cylinder Gas Division of Chemetron Corp. in Chicago, Illinois.

WHAT A YEAR IT WAS

ARE THE STARS OUT TONIGHT?

Hughes Aircraft in Culver City, California has invented a laser rangefinder, "Colidar Mark II," which can be handled as easily as a rifle for use in pinpointing military targets by measuring distances.

ALBERT A. FAULKNER INVENTS "NOVA III," A MODERATE-PRICED PLANETARIUM DESIGNED FOR USE IN SCHOOLS AND SMALL COLLEGES.

A new sonic detector developed by the **Illinois Institute of Technology** makes it possible to detect gas leaks in mains without disturbing large areas of street surface.

THIS WON'T BE A SHATTERING EXPERIENCE

Pittsburgh Plate Glass is in production with a high-strength, tempered safety glass designed for use in schools and homes.

SHEDDING SOME LIGHT ON THE SUBJECT

Power Sales Co. out of Ardmore, Pennsylvania is marketing a new screwdriver that illuminates hard-to see places.

TRY CHANGING THIS ONE

Goodyear Tire & Rubber has produced the world's largest tire, 10 feet tall and almost 4 feet wide, which will be used on an oil-well drilling rig in the U.S.

Friction welding is invented.

LONG-DISTANCE DIAGNOSIS OF BRAIN DISORDERS IS NOW A POSSIBILITY FOLLOWING THE EXPERIMENTAL TRANSMISSION OF BRAIN WAVES VIA SATELLITE FROM BRISTOL, ENGLAND TO MINNEAPOLIS, MINNESOTA.

NETTING A NEW RACKET

Former French tennis champion Rene Lacoste patents a revolutionary tennis racquet with a steel frame rather than wood.

WHAT A YEAR IT WAS!

Advanced Unit Construction with massive one-piece uniside

Bucket seats, console, Twin-Stick Floor Shift

Room for six 6-footers

1963 Rambler Classic Six "770" 4-Door Sedan. Available with 198-hp V-8 engine.

Floor shift, bucket seats, console, headrests optional.

Rambler wins 1963 Motor Trend "Car of the Year" Award

America's most wanted automotive honor, the coveted "Car of the Year" Award from *Motor Trend Magazine*, goes to Rambler '63 over all other cars. Big reason: A whole host of new and major Rambler betterments which are available in no other cars.

Most important betterment is all-new Advanced Unit Construction in Rambler Classic Six or V-8, and in Ambassador V-8—a years-ahead breakthrough in car building. It provides vastly increased strength—permits long, flowing lines in a car almost 3 inches

lower, yet with full headroom for six 6-footers, amazingly easier entrance and exit, with curved glass side windows that permit doors to curve into the roof.

A major advance in power transfer—Tri-Poised Power—brings new velvet smoothness at all speeds. The entire car is so trouble-free and service-free, it's the longest-lasting Rambler ever.

Come see and try the '63 Ramblers—the most beautiful Ramblers ever built—now at your Rambler dealer.
American Motors—Dedicated To Excellence

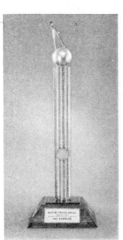

Rambler awarded 1963
CAR OF THE YEAR
Trophy by
Motor Trend Magazine

RAMBLER '63   THE NEW SHAPE OF QUALITY

134

[SCIENCE] — 1963

YOU MEAN IT DOESN'T COME DOWN??

Communist Party newspaper *Pravda* reports the discovery of a new physical law that corrects the laws of Sir Isaac Newton.

DOUBLESPEAK
NO MORE

100 scientists representing 22 information committees in the U.S. establish the SCIENTISTS' INSTITUTE FOR PUBLIC INFORMATION for the purpose of providing the public with objective, understandable scientific information.

According to a theory put forth at the American Physical Society by Ernest J. Sternglass of Westinghouse Research Laboratories, all matter is electricity and is composed not of 30 or more elementary particles, but only of two – the negatively charged electron and its counterpart, the positively charged positron.

AT&T and the British post office kick off the first direct trans-atlantic submarine telephone cable between the U.S. and England.

A record low temperature of 143°C is measured at an altitude of about 50 miles in noctilucent clouds over Swedish Lapland, confirming the theory that these cloud particles are coated with ice.

Barnes Engineering Co. produces the **thermogram**, a singular camera that will detect cancerous hot spots.

After discovering that condensation from human breath has produced microscopic vegetation in the cave's ancient paintings, French authorities close Lascaux Cave for treatment to halt the deterioration.

NOBEL PRIZES

PHYSIOLOGY or MEDICINE

Sir John C. Eccles
(Australia)

Alan L. Hodgkin
(Great Britain)

Andrew F. Huxley
(Great Britain)

PHYSICS

Eugene Wigner
(U.S.A.)

Maria Goeppert-Mayer
(U.S.A.)

J. Hans D. Jensen
(Germany)

CHEMISTRY

Karl Ziegler
(Germany)

Giulio Natta
(Italy)

California's Institute of Technology claims the discovery that gold, platinum, iron, uranium and other heavy chemical elements of the earth were formed 6-10 billion years before the creation of the earth's solar system and are 10-15 billion years old.

DR. HELGE INGSTAD EXCAVATES A VIKING VILLAGE BUILT IN A.D. 1000 IN NEWFOUNDLAND, INDICATING THE ROUTE USED BY NORSEMEN.

ARE YOU MY LONG-LOST BROTHER?

LOUIS S. B. LEAKEY DISCOVERS THE SKULL OF AN APELIKE CREATURE ESTIMATED TO BE 14,000,000 YEARS OLD WITH A CANINE TOOTH AND MUSCLE ANCHORAGE CLOSER TO THE HUMAN FORM THAN THAT OF APES.

The U.S. Court of Appeals in Washington upholds a lower-court decision denying a plea by DR. LINUS C. PAULING for a court order to halt tests producing radiation.

Dr. Linus C. Pauling

Nobel Peace Prize winner DR. LINUS C. PAULING attacks the lunar program, calling it *"a pitiful demonstration"* and that *"something is wrong with our system of values when we plan to spend billions of dollars for national prestige"* and *"the money should be spent on combating disease and human suffering."*

atomic NEWS 1963

The Navy launches its 51st nuclear submarine, the ULYSSES S. GRANT, in Groton, Connecticut.

Director of the Institute for Advanced Studies, Dr. J. Robert Oppenheimer is given the AEC's $50,000 Enrico Fermi Award for his contributions to nuclear energy.

J. Robert Oppenheimer receives award from President Lyndon Johnson.

The *Physical Review Letters* announces the discovery of the 34th and last elementary particle in the atomic nucleus, the anti-Xi-zero.

A new family of atomic particles called "W" particles, representing one of the four fundamental forces of nature, is discovered at the International Atomic Research Center in Switzerland.

DOUBLE TROUBLE

U.S. reports that the atomic tests conducted last year by the Soviet Union and the U.S. doubled the world's radioactive debris.

According to the Russian newspaper *Pravda*, the Kurchatov Institute of Atomic Energy has produced stable plasma at a temperature of 40 million degrees C and density of 10 million particles per cubic cm.

Ohio receives its first electricity from atomic energy at the AEC's nuclear plant in Piqua, the first nuclear facility to use an organic cooled and moderated reactor and the first nuclear plant of any type to be operated by a municipal utility company.

WHAT A YEAR IT WAS!

Outer Space

Pay Now, Fly Later

A Lockheed study conducted for NASA concludes that in 10 years there could be an operating passenger shuttle between earth and a space station, with the fare as little as $25,000.

- - - - - - -

Earth satellite **Explorer 17** is launched from Cape Canaveral.

- - - - - - -

Two satellites designed to detect man-made nuclear explosions in space are launched from Cape Canaveral.

- - - - - - -

For the first time, using just three geosynchronous communications satellites that send and receive messages to each other and earth, most of the world can stay in continuous contact thanks to the newly launched satellite, **Syncom II**.

- - - - - - -

The ailing TV satellites **Telstar 1** and **Relay 1** are back in operation, relaying transatlantic TV signals successfully.

- - - - - - -

Tiros 8, a 265-pound weather satellite, is launched from Cape Kennedy (formerly Cape Canaveral).

- - - - - - -

The General Accounting Office charges that NASA and private contractors have mismanaged U.S. space projects, delaying the lunar program by two years with a cost of $100 million in federal money.

- - - - - - -

An orbiting U.S. satellite is the first to use a nuclear generator as its only source of electricity.

NASA launches a satellite.

138

The Astronauts

Neil A. Armstrong
Frank Borman
Malcolm Scott Carpenter
Charles Conrad, Jr.
L. Gordon Cooper, Jr.
John H. Glenn, Jr.
Virgil I. Grissom
James A. Lovell
James A. McDivitt
Wally M. Schirra, Jr.
Elliot M. See, Jr.
Alan B. Shepard, Jr.
Donald K. Slayton
Thomas P. Stafford
Edward H. White
John W. Young

In the last MERCURY flight, **Major L. Gordon Cooper** completes America's longest manned spaceflight when he pilots his MERCURY capsule to a landing in the Pacific Ocean after 22 orbits around the earth. The automatic control system fails during reentry and Cooper guides FAITH 7 to splashdown, 4.5 miles from target. He is the fourth American and eighth human being known to have gone into orbit.

- - - - - - -

Air Force Capt. **Edward J. Dwight, Jr.** is the first black chosen for astronaut training.

TWIN ORBITS

The Soviets score another space first as Junior Lieutenant **Valentina Tereshkova** becomes the first spacewoman to achieve orbit, making 48 revolutions in her *Vostok VI* capsule at the same time Soviet cosmonaut **Valery Bykovsky** is orbiting the earth.

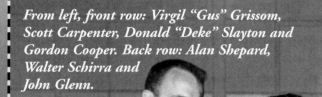

From left, front row: Virgil "Gus" Grissom, Scott Carpenter, Donald "Deke" Slayton and Gordon Cooper. Back row: Alan Shepard, Walter Schirra and John Glenn.

JUST A BIT WARM FOR SUNBATHING

Interplanetary probe MARINER 2 reports Venus has surface temperatures of around 800°F and is covered by cold dense clouds in the upper atmosphere.

O.K. – WHAT ABOUT JUPITER?

A telescope with a balloon is sent up to explore if life can be supported on Mars, and preliminary findings indicate life on Mars would be marginal at best.

Scientists from around the world converge on the North American continent to observe the total solar eclipse of July 20.

Most meteoroids appear to be flakes of fluff from decaying meteors rather than solid bits of rock and metal, according to Dr. Fred L. Whipple, director of Harvard's Smithsonian Astrophysical Observatory, and should not endanger future space travelers.

WE'LL TAKE SOME NEEDLING ON THIS ONE

400 million copper dipoles (needles), each about 3/4 inch long and about one-third the thickness of a human hair, have been successfully released in space by a U.S. Air Force satellite.

Confirmation of the existence of X rays in the direction of the Crab Nebula and the Scorpio constellation is confirmed by USAF rocket shots.

The Mt. Wilson and Mt. Palomar observatories report the discovery of the five brightest objects in the universe – with two of these radio galaxies being at least 100 times brighter than our Milky Way.

Mt. Wilson observatory

The U.S. and U.S.S.R. give final approval to an agreement calling for cooperation in weather, communications and magnetic satellite programs.

A joint venture between the U.S. and U.S.S.R. to make indirect measurements of cosmic rays of the sun by studying changes in radio reception is announced by the National Science Foundation.

Soviet Premier Nikita Khrushchev announces that *"at the present time we do not plan flights of cosmonauts to the moon."*

The Soviet Union announces that their scientists bounced a radio signal off the planet Jupiter and that the 745-million-mile round-trip took one hour, six minutes.

Medicine

THINGS COULD BE HEATING UP

While steam baths or saunas might feel good, they have no medical benefits and in fact can be harmful to people with hardening of the arteries, heart disorders or overactive thyroids.

I MAY BE OLDER, BUT I AIN'T DUMBER

Results of neuropsychological testing of 10,000 people at the University of Chicago reveal that brain power does not diminish with age up to 50 and that it does not necessarily decrease after that.

A report in the NEW ENGLAND JOURNAL OF MEDICINE contradicts a popular profile of potential heart attack victims, currently described as tense, driving, ambitious men in responsible jobs. Research of 122 men and 11 women under 50 who died of a heart attack indicates that their jobs involved little or no stress and are characterized as living more sedentary lives consisting of watching television, reading and visiting family and friends. Ten men and three women were found to be alcoholics.

HAVE A HANKERING TO **EAT A BOX OF SOAP?**

Cravings for odd items may be caused by a nutritional deficiency or a glandular disorder, so the next time you want to chew on a hunk of wood, see your doctor first.

CONSCIOUSNESS EXPANSION OR **INSANITY?**

An editorial appearing in the *Archives of General Psychiatry* by Dr. Roy R. Grinker, Sr. warns about the indiscriminate use of LSD-25, which could cause serious mental illness and even death.

WHAT EXACTLY **DOES THIS SCRIBBLE MEAN?**

Research director of Methodist Hospital in Gary, Indiana claims that illegible penmanship by doctors and nurses is costing hospitals thousands of dollars in deciphering time.

Are you using the most modern way to relieve hemorrhoids?

You can be sure—with The PAZO Formula in convenient suppository form . . . most modern way to shrink hemorrhoid tissue without surgery. Here's why . . .

MODERN IN FORM. PAZO suppositories are ideal for today's active people. Foil-wrapped, handy to carry in pocket or purse, simple to use wherever you go. Stainless, pure-white . . . no messy applicator, no messy stains.

MODERN IN FORMULA. Some products claim all-purpose ingredients which are expected to do many jobs. PAZO suppositories, however, are a scientifically developed *combination* of tested ingredients . . . each chosen for its ability to do one *primary* job with full-strength effectiveness.

Primary Function of Specific Ingredient	PAZO	Most Heavily Advertised Brand	Petroleum Jelly
Pile Tissue Shrinkage	X	X	
Lubrication	X	X	X
Antiseptic Action	X	X	
Pain Relief	X		
Itch Relief	X		

Use the most modern way to soothe and shrink hemorrhoid tissue without surgery . . . PAZO suppositories. Ask for . . .

MAD ABOUT THAT BIG DRIP?

"YES!" — not only annoying but can waste 8000 gal. water QUARTERLY — DOUBLE WATER, FUEL, UPKEEP bills!

Most faucet leaks are the result of washers fastened with TOO SHORT or TOO LONG screws — that quickly loosen and cause DRIP.

THE S-O-L-U-T-I-O-N!

★ Now—the NEW 'Sexauer' SELF-LOCKING MONEL SCREW — with embedded, expanding NYLOK® PLUG that LOCKS at required depth AUTOMATICALLY — HOLDS WASHER FIRMLY!

★ Used with N-E-W, HEAT-RESIST-ING, 'Sexauer' EASY-TITE WASHER — P-R-E-V-E-N-T-S swelling that chokes off water's flow — WHILE OUTWEARING ordinary washers "6-to-1"!

Note Nylok® Plug —locks screws automatically

Note Fiberglas backing—resists closing squeeze
®T.M. Reg. U. S. Pat. Off.
The Nylok Corporation

Only "1-IN-10" Plumbers are 'SEXAUER' AUTHORIZED, QUALITY DEALERS, who carry "OVER 4000" 'SEXAUER' TRIPLE-WEAR REPAIR PARTS, including WORLD FAMOUS M-U-L-E K-I-C-K products for pepping up sluggish drains, restoring glisten to TOILET BOWLS — and lustre to chrome bath and kitchen fixtures. *For "1-IN-10" Sexauer QUALITY AUTHORIZED DEALER in your neighborhood—WRITE:*

J. A. SEXAUER MFG. CO., INC., DEPT. AS-53
10 HAMILTON AVE., WHITE PLAINS, N. Y.

The American Heart Association is the first voluntary public agency to launch a drive against cigarette smoking.

The California Medical Association is the first state medical association to publicly declare that cigarette smoking is a health hazard.

The American Cancer Society releases a report linking cigarette smoking and early death from diseases including lung cancer and heart disease.

The U.S. Surgeon General releases report on smoking with the following conclusions:

- Smoking is a major cause of lung and larynx cancer, as well as bronchitis.
- Cigarette smoke is a greater cause of chest problems than smog or other air pollution.
- Smokers have a higher death rate from heart disease and blood vessel problems than nonsmokers.

The Florida Supreme Court upholds the ruling of the U.S. District Court that cigarettes had caused cancer and holds that a cigarette manufacturer can be held liable if a person's death is caused by the company's product.

Study Goes Up In Smoke

Unable to staff a study committee, the American Medical Association cancels its planned one-year study of the "possible causal relationship of tobacco use and the development of various diseases."

No Midnight Raids On The Ashtray

Smoking cessation clinics in Stockholm are treating people with a combination of nicotine injections and education.

The AMA recommends that people with medical conditions requiring specific treatment wear a bracelet, anklet or medallion available through the Medic Alert Foundation.

IT'S ALL MOM & DAD'S FAULT

An associate professor at the University of Illinois says that about one out of every ten people suffers from migraine headaches and usually the headache is hereditary.

The U.S. Public Health Service says evidence indicates that upper respiratory diseases, including the common cold, occur more frequently in areas suffering from air pollution.

NOTHING TO SNEEZE AT

A Kansas City doctor says that ragweed alone is not the cause of hay fever but that other fall pollinating plants or molds and foods could cause allergic responses.

LET'S GET UN-STONED

A new organic solvent has been developed that appears to be effective in dissolving and preventing kidney stones.

According to the American Cancer Society, an estimated 1.2 million people have whipped cancer, showing no evidence of disease for at least five years after completion of treatment.

 ## YOU CAN SEE CLEARLY NOW

An ophthalmologist at the University of Minnesota reports that cataract surgery has a very high success rate.

FINDING THOSE HOT SPOTS

A new device in operation at the National Institutes of Health in Bethesda, Maryland is capable of recording the amount of radiation in 18 different sections of the body.

Specialists in the field of tissue transplantation predict that replacing diseased or worn-out hearts, kidneys, lungs and livers with healthy organs will usher in a golden age of surgery within 25 years.

GIVING A NEW MEANING TO: "WHAT DO YOU WANT? BLOOD?"

To help eliminate dangerous reactions to blood transfusions, doctors at Augustana Hospital and the State Tuberculosis Hospital in Chicago have patients donate their own blood in advance of surgery.

Dr. Margaret J. Albrink of the West Virginia University School of Medicine indicates that triglycerides, important but relatively unknown fats in the blood, may actually provide a much better indicator of coronary artery disease than cholesterol.

Half the people who develop heart disease die within three weeks – many within one hour.

THE OPERATION WAS SUCCESSFUL, BUT THE PATIENT DIED

The first successful human liver transplant is performed at the Veterans Hospital in Denver, but the patient dies 22 days later of pneumonia.

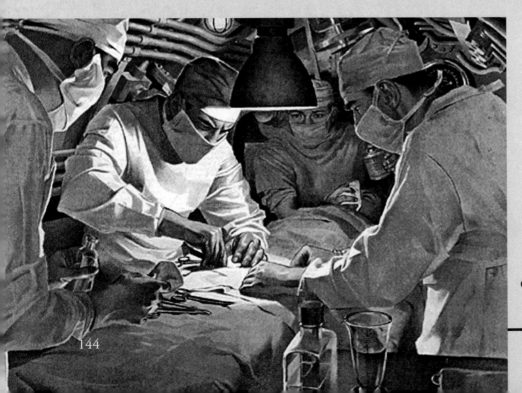

Surgeons at the University of Mississippi Hospital successfully perform a revolutionary lung transplant, but the patient, serving life in prison, dies a short time later of kidney failure.

Dr. Michael De Bakey is the first to use an artificial heart to take over the circulation of a patient's blood during heart surgery, but the patient dies four days later from complications.

WHAT A YEAR IT WAS!

The FDA rejects the use of Krebiozen for the treatment of cancer.

•

The AMA issues a policy statement approving the use of a synthetic drug for up to three weeks in the treatment of drug addicts.

•

In an effort to avoid another thalidomide disaster, the FDA issues new drug-testing regulations.

•

The University of Chicago Clinics claims *"measurable and clinically worth-while improvement"* in 15 patients with breast cancer, using two female hormones, a combination of estradiol and progesterone.

•

The FDA announces that Enovid, a progesterone hormone used to suppress ovulation, is safe when used as directed but warns against its use by women over 34 years of age.

•

Using a hormone made from human pituitary glands, two undersized girls have increased their height, according to doctors at the University of Wisconsin Medical School.

Following the U.S. Food & Drug Administration's ruling calling for tighter regulations on the marketing of drugs, 37 U.S. drug companies file suit, charging that the new labels and ads would be confusing to doctors and cost the drug firms in excess of $1 million to destroy and replace present literature.

•

Roche introduces Valium following FDA approval.

•

The Surgeon General urges vaccination of infants aged nine months to one year, with the federal government licensing two measles vaccines – a killed-virus by Pfizer & Co. and a live-virus by Merck Sharp & Dohme.

•

The Surgeon General's office licenses the three-in-one oral polio vaccine developed by Albert Sabin and Herald R. Cox after seven years of testing.

•

Claiming that it is highly addictive, California State Attorney General Stanley Mosk urges the FDA to investigate the drug Percodan.

NO NEW WRINKLE FOR THOSE OLD WRINKLES

A report out of Boston University School of Medicine indicates that despite advertising claims, there is no scientific evidence to show that hormone cosmetics remove wrinkles.

TAKE AN ASPIRIN AND CALL YOUR LAWYER IN THE MORNING

The FTC charges Bayer Aspirin maker Sterling Drug and its advertising agency Dancer-Fitzgerald-Sample with falsely advertising that Bayer Aspirin is superior to other pain relievers.

A WIGGY SUBJECT

A New York dermatologist predicts that within a decade a synthetic female hormone will be developed to prevent female baldness.

Originally introduced as a means of preventing tooth decay, Dr. Frederick J. Stare of the Harvard School of Public Health states that fluoridated water is providing an added bonus in the form of stronger bones for older people by influencing the deposit of calcium in the bones, thus helping to retard osteoporosis.

WHAT A YEAR IT WAS!

The Mamas

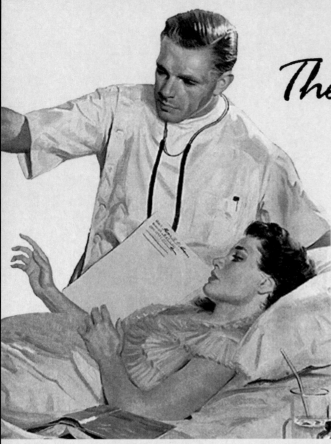

Hair loss that occurs in women following childbirth generally grows back in five to six months.

A Harvard University research team reveals that there is a danger of mental disease for new mothers and it usually will manifest during the first three months after the birth of the baby, with mothers in their 30s having the smallest risk of developing manic-depressive psychoses.

Motherhood - It Ain't All It's Cracked Up To Be

Half of all new mothers interviewed by Dr. Sheila C. Mitchell of the Department of Obstetrics at the University of Michigan Medical Center suffered a *"disenchantment syndrome"* shortly after returning home with their child and felt an *"unexpected depression and a sense of being trapped within the house."*

The American College of Obstetricians and Gynecologists passes a resolution fully approving the dissemination of birth control information to anyone who requests it.

New York physician Dr. Wolfgang A. Casper advises that strawberry marks be removed immediately at birth.

FIRST THE EYES, NOW THE FEET

Children sitting in a squat position in front of the television set run the risk of developing foot trouble and could take on a pigeon-toe or toe-in position in walking.

Young boys with asthma generally observe sports rather than participate.

Treating both parents of emotionally disturbed children has met with considerable success at the Flint Child Guidance Clinic at the Michigan State University Psychological Clinic.

GET OUT THOSE EARPLUGS

A Florida family physician with a large pediatric practice advises that to avoid childhood tantrums and teenage emotional disturbances, babies should experience *"small doses of frustration"* by the parents not meeting their every demand immediately.

In the opinion of Dr. Orval R. Withers of the University of Kansas Medical School, many foods are the cause of food allergies because of the drugs, chemicals or antibiotics used in food processing.

DRINK, DRINK, PERCHANCE TO DREAM

Drinking coffee at bedtime won't necessarily keep you awake, says the American Medical Association, if you are a regular coffee drinker, and in fact a cup of coffee may actually relax the tense, anxious individual and act as a sleep aid.

BETTER RETHINK THAT SECOND CUP OF JOE

Studies conducted at a Western Electric Company plant in Cicero, Illinois indicate a direct correlation between heart disease and drinking coffee.

WHAT A YEAR IT WAS!

SCRATCHING THE SURFACE

Dr. Farrington Daniels, Jr., of Cornell University Medical College, contends that a patient with a generalized itching problem is generally treated by society with hilarity.

THANK GOD... THE STOCK MARKET WENT DOWN AGAIN TODAY

According to Dr. Henry Krystal, assistant professor of psychiatry at Wayne State University College of Medicine, if you've been consistently losing money in the stock market, you may need a good analyst to determine if you unconsciously want to lose your money to atone for unresolved guilt.

"RED HERRING" is a label doctors apply to a patient who unintentionally withholds his real reason for the visit, which could mean the patient is trying to avoid anxiety, shame or guilt about his actual needs.

GOLF can be an excellent arena for working out conflict, widening ego activity, working through infantile neurosis and may become neurotic behavior itself.

HELLO, IS THIS A SHRINK TO WHOM I AM SPEAKING?

The Philadelphia Mental Health Clinic inaugurates a dial-a-psychiatrist emergency service allowing a patient to reach a psychiatrist by phone 24 hours a day.

STRAIGHT OUT OF THE STRAIGHT JACKET AND INTO A PILL

Many medical authorities are concerned about the possible overuse of tranquilizers in mental hospitals.

TAKE A DRUG – FORGET YOUR FEARS

A University of Michigan psychiatrist says the effectiveness of drugs for treating mental illness has been exaggerated and has emptied our psychiatric wards without offering patients continuing, definitive treatment.

HONEY, COME AND GET YOUR HUGS

The head of health and physical education at Chicago's George Williams College says that giving your wife a big hug for five seconds every morning not only encourages marital bliss, but provides good exercise as well.

SCOTCH ON THE ROCKS & LOVE IN THE AFTERNOON

A report given to the Eastern Psychological Association indicates that social drinking increases a man's thoughts of love, sex and romance and diminishes restraint and sense of time.

Now right in your own office...
COPY EVERYTHING
Faster, Easier, at Lower Cost than Ever Before!

COPIES EVERYTHING
Crayon *Pen*
Pencil *Ball Point*
TYPEWRITER *Printing*
Every Color
Every Paper

NEW APĒCO ELECTRO-STAT
AUTOMATIC • ELECTRONICALLY DRY

Now, the new APECO ELECTRO-STAT gives you faster, sharper copies every time. It copies everything...electronically dry! Copies are error-proof, legally accepted; never fade or discolor. In addition, any copy can be used as an offset master to make quantity copies at less than 1/5¢ each. Fits on the corner of any desk, anywhere in your office...eliminates the costly walking and waiting of a centralized copying department. And, with all its operating speed and efficiency the ELECTRO-STAT is priced well within the budget of every firm!

send for FREE BOOKLET

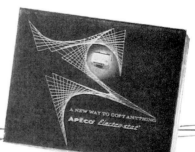

Mail the attached reply card to receive New Free book that shows the many advantages of Electro-static copying for your business.

BUSINESS

THE NUMBERS

Total 1963 income for Americans is over $400 billion.

- - -

A whopping $105.9 billion in taxes is collected by the IRS during fiscal 1963. It is not only a record for the U.S., but for the entire world.
New Yorkers pay the most of any state, at $19.1 billion.

- - -

The hourly minimum wage is raised from $1.15 to $1.25.

- - -

The Gross National Product is $585 billion.

- - -

The average unemployment figure is 5.6% – four million people.

STOP THE PRESSES. FOREVER.

The NEW YORK MIRROR, the second biggest newspaper in the country, calls it quits after 39 years.

- - -

France vetoes Great Britain's entrance into the European Economic Community.

On November 15, President Kennedy states that *"jobs are the most important domestic issue that this country faces,"* more so than education or civil rights.

President Kennedy signs into law a bill providing equal pay for equal work, thus benefiting the millions of underpaid women across the nation.

1963

STOCKS

A record 1,147,183,295 shares are traded on the New York Stock Exchange.

The Dow-Jones reaches a record high of 767.21. The low for the year is 646.79.

The Federal Reserve Board increases the margin requirement to purchase securities listed on stock exchanges from 50 to 70%.

After President Kennedy's assassination, and before the emergency shutdown of the New York Stock Exchange, panic causes over two million shares to be traded while the Dow-Jones drops 21 points. A record $15 billion is traded the first day the Exchange reopens, while the Dow-Jones rises a record 32 points.

Stock prices grow about 17%.

ROLLIN', ROLLIN', ROLLIN', KEEP THOSE CARS A ROLLIN'

Willys Motors, Inc. becomes **Kaiser Jeep Corp.**

7,644,110 cars are built during the year in the U.S., with **Chevrolet** remaining the #1 automaker for the fourth year in a row.

Studebaker Corporation installs seat belts in all cars made after March 1.

In December, **Studebaker Corporation** announces it will end manufacturing in the U.S. by closing its South Bend, Indiana plant.

Ford Motor Company
 . . . makes its 60 millionth vehicle.
 . . . turns 60.

SEARS ROEBUCK & CO.'S

earnings during December are bigger than any other month in the company's 77 years.

THAT'S A LOT OF COPIES

Earnings for **XEROX** Corporation surpass $23 million.

A MATCH MADE IN HEAVEN

With combined assets of over $3 billion, Crocker-Anglo National Bank of San Francisco merges with Citizens National Bank of Los Angeles, becoming Crocker-Citizens National Bank.

PRIME-TIME BUCKS

Chairman of the Board William S. Paley sells 75,000 shares of his CBS stock for over $3 1/2 million.

UNION NEWS

FEWER PEOPLE STRIKE THAN ANY OTHER POSTWAR YEAR.

TWO OF THE LONGEST – AND MOST EXPENSIVE – NEWSPAPER STRIKES FINALLY COME TO A CLOSE.

Where's All The News That's Fit To Print?

At times the 114-day New York strike, which started in 1962, affects all seven of Manhattan's papers plus two on Long Island. Roughly $108 million is lost by the companies in ad revenue and home deliveries. One aftereffect of the strike is the doubling of the *New York Times'* price from 5¢ to 10¢.

The Cleveland, Ohio strike, which also began in 1962, stops after 129 days, costing the *Cleveland Press* and the *Plain Dealer* in the neighborhood of $25 million.

JOHN L. LEWIS retires as Chairman of the Board of the National Coal Policy Conference, Inc.

At the AFL-CIO convention, President **GEORGE MEANY** calls automation a *"curse to society."*

John L. Lewis

The AFL-CIO Executive Council passes a resolution calling for a 35-hour workweek and more money for overtime.

A labor agreement is reached between AFL-CIO United Steelworkers of America and 11 steel companies without a strike.

and he works for bananas

Australian farmer Lindsay Schmidt uses his monkey to drive a tractor and other odd jobs, leaving local union bureaucrats unsure if the monkey is eligible for union membership.

FOOD BASKET

Apples (lb.)	$ .10
Avocados (each)	.14
Bell Peppers (lb.)	.08
Bread (loaf)	.33
Broccoli (lb.)	.19
Butter (lb.)	.69
Cantaloupe (lb.)	.05
Cheddar Cheese (lb.)	.59
Coffee (lb.)	.89
Cottage Cheese (pt.)	.25
Cream Cheese	.35
Cucumbers (each)	.05
Eggs (dz.)	.45
Graham Crackers	.29
Grapes (lb.)	.10
Grapefruit (lb.)	.10

Ice Cream (1/2 gallon)	$ .59
Lemons (lb.)	.10
Lettuce (head)	.17
Milk (qt.)	.27
Olive Oil	.31
Pound Cake	.39
Peanut Butter	.49
Tomatoes (lb.)	.15

☐ YEARLY SALARIES ☐

Accountant	$ 8,000
Architect	19,000
Art Director	12,000
Bank Teller	5,100
Chemist	12,000
Congressman	25,000
Copywriter	7,000
Engineer	11,500
Factory Worker	5,200
Government Employee	5,200
Insurance Agent	8,500
Military Personnel	4,000
Pilot	28,000
President of the United States	100,000
Secretary	4,700
Tax Attorney	9,000
Teachers:	
National Average	5,735
Highest State Average – Alaska	7,350
Lowest State Average – Arkansas	3,737
Highest City Average – Beverly Hills, CA	up to 14,000
Television Industry	8,000
Travel Agent	6,000

THE STOCK MARKET

The average price of a share on the New York Stock Exchange is $50.73.

Alaska Airlines	4	Hilton Hotels	22 1/2
Boeing	34 1/8	Loews Theater	18
CBS	76 1/4	Macy's	64
Chrysler	90	Mattel	52
Coca-Cola	103 3/4	Maytag	38 1/8
Decca	45 1/2	Motorola	67 1/2
Disney	44	Pfizer	50
General Telephone	27	Pillsbury	56
Gerber	66 1/2	Safeway	60
Hewlett Packard	22	Texaco	70 1/2

AROUND THE HOUSE

Alka Seltzer	$ .59
Aspirin (100)	.53
Baby Powder	.89
Baby Stroller	12.88
Bobby Pins (20)	.01
Broom	.98
Brownie Camera	18.95
Deodorant	.79
Dishtowel	.29
Disposable Diapers	1.98
Hair Dryer	17.88
Hair Spray	.99
High Chair	10.88
Infant Car Seat	4.98
Lysol	1.19
Mop	.99
Refrigerator	198.00

1963

Television	$ 449.00
Tissues	.39
Toothpaste	.69
Transistor Radio	14.95
Walkie-Talkie	4.44

THIS & THAT

Bicycle	$ 47.95
Film Admission	.85
Guitar	39.95
Hospital, Average Daily Rate	36.83
Long-Distance Phone Call (3 minutes)	1.00
New York City Subway Token	.15
Stamp	.05
Train Ride, L.A. to Denver	42.98

THE MRS. SHOP

Boots	$ 14.98
Bra	3.95
Designer Suit	160.00
Diamond Ring (1 carat)	235.00
Dress	17.98
Gloves	7.99
Hat	4.98
Lipstick	1.25
Nail Polish	.75
Nightgown	1.98
Permanent & Haircut	22.50
Sweater	20.88

THE MR. SHOP

Cashmere Overcoat	$ 119.95
Pajamas	3.99
Polo Shirt	5.00
Shaving Cream	$ .79
Shirt	10.50
Slacks	16.95
Socks	1.29
Suit	65.00
Sweater	25.00
Tie	5.00
Tiffany Watch	985.00
Underwear	2.95

HOME SWEET HOME

3-Bedroom House National Average	$ 12,000
Memphis, Tennessee	8,675
Chicago, Illinois	16,250
Teaneck, New Jersey	24,990
New Canaan, Connecticut	35,000
Great Neck, New York	39,990
Pacific Palisades, California	52,500

Fun-savers for '63 ...from Kodak!

Don't <u>spend</u> your summer weekends— <u>save</u> them with an easy-to-use Kodak camera!

Easy to carry, easy to use! Weighs less than eight ounces including new compact, built-in flash! No need to focus. Takes sharp, clear snapshots or slides from as close as 4 feet. **BROWNIE STARMITE II Camera** . . . less than $12.

(Complete gift outfit less than $14.)

Built-in exposure meter measures light, tells you the correct lens setting for every shot. Sharp *f*/8 lens never needs focusing. Attractive, lightweight, moderately priced. **BROWNIE STARMETER Camera** . . . less than $23.

(Complete gift outfit less than $29.)

35mm precision — snapshot ease! Shutter speeds to a fast 1/250 of a second! Easy focusing, *f*/2.8 lens. Takes sharp, clear slides or snapshots as close as 3½ feet. **KODAK RETINETTE 1A Camera** . . . less than $49.

Prices subject to change without notice.

Shows up to 36 slides without trays! Smooth push-pull changing, easy editing. Brilliant 500-watt lamp, *f*/3.5 lens. Sturdy self-case—no case to buy! **KODAK READYMATIC 500 Projector** . . . less than $70.

Be prepared for the fun—with plenty of KODAK Film! You can *depend* on the name Kodak.

P.S. Ask your dealer to show you the newest Kodak Fun-saver the **Kodak Instamatic** Camera with **Kodapak** Film Cartridge!

EASTMAN KODAK COMPANY, ROCHESTER 4, N.Y.

DISASTERS

NATURAL DISASTERS

A tidal wave hits **Chittagong, East Pakistan** and other regions on the Bay of Bengal, taking the lives of 11,500 people.

•

Hurricane Flora kills approximately 5,000 in **Haiti** and 1,000 in **Cuba**.

•

Three separate eruptions within three months of Mt. Agung in **Bali, Indonesia** take the lives of roughly 1,600 people.

•

In **Skopje, Yugoslavia** an earthquake kills 1,030 people and nearly levels the city in only 30 seconds.

•

Across Europe, 400 die from snowstorms.

•

Around 200 die when a landslide near **Kathmandu, Nepal** destroys several villages.

FLOODS

Piave River Valley, Italy:	**2,200 dead**
Uttar Pradesh, India:	**237 dead**
Herat, Afghanistan:	**107 dead**
Northern Morocco:	**100 dead**
Ohio River Valley:	**17 dead**

1963

AIRPLANE CRASHES

Quebec, Canada:	118 dead
Southeastern Alaska:	101 dead
(military personnel and their families)	
Elkton, Maryland:	82 dead
Duerrenaesch, Switzerland:	80 dead
Douala, Cameroon:	54 dead
Everglades, Florida:	43 dead
São Paulo, Brazil:	41 dead
Perpignan, France:	40 dead

U.S. HOLIDAY TRAFFIC DEATH TOLLS

Memorial Day: 159

July 4: 510
(record)

Labor Day: 556

FIRE TRAGEDIES

A nursing home is destroyed by a fire that kills 63 near **Fitchville, Ohio**.

In **Diourbel, Senegal** a fire in a movie theater kills 64 people.

An explosion caused by propane gas kills 72 people and injures hundreds during a "Holiday on Ice" show at the State Fairgrounds Coliseum in **Indianapolis, Indiana**.

ASSORTED CATASTROPHES

250 die when the ferry *Djandji Radja* sinks in North Sumatra, Indonesia.

452 coal miners die in Omuta, Japan from an explosion while approximately 450 are injured.

In the worst U.S. naval submarine calamity, the U.S.S. *Thresher*, a nuclear sub, disappears after making a dive in the North Atlantic with 129 men on board.

WHAT A YEAR IT WAS!

SPORTS

BASEBALL

WORLD SERIES

Los Angeles Dodgers over New York Yankees, 4-0

MVP

Sandy Koufax, LA

CY YOUNG AWARD

Sandy Koufax, LA

Batting Champions

National League
Tommy Davis (LA, .326)

American League
Carl Yastrzemski (Boston, .321)

Strikeouts

National League
Sandy Koufax (LA, 306)

American League
Camilo Pascual (Minnesota, 202)

Stolen Bases

National League
Maury Wills (LA, 40)

American League
Luis Aparicio (Baltimore, 40)

THE ALL-STAR GAME

National over American, 5-3

Home Run Leaders

National League
Hank Aaron (Milwaukee, 44)
Willie McCovey (SF, 44)

American League
Harmon Killebrew (Minnesota, 45)

Most Valuable Player

National League
Sandy Koufax (LA)

American League
Elston Howard (NY)

WILLIE MAYS, 31-year-old San Francisco Giants outfielder, signs a new one-year contract for an estimated $100,000, making him baseball's highest-paid player.

31-year-old N.Y. Yankees outfielder **MICKEY MANTLE** signs his 1963 contract for $100,000, becoming the fifth player to earn this salary.

Outfielder/first baseman with the St. Louis Cardinals for 22 years, **STAN MUSIAL** announces his retirement at the end of the current season. 42-year-old Musial set or tied 17 Major League records, 30 National League records, 9 All-Star game records, held 7 batting titles and was voted the League's Most Valuable Player 3 times.

Los Angeles Dodgers pitcher **SANDY KOUFAX** sets World Series strikeout record with 15 in a single game.

PRESIDENT KENNEDY kicks off the baseball season by tossing out the first ball at Washington's District of Columbia Stadium game between the Washington Senators and the Baltimore Orioles.

RALPH HOUK takes over as general manager of the N.Y. Yankees and **YOGI BERRA** (*pictured*) is named new manager.

THE DEPENDABLES BUILT BY DODGE!

GO FOR THE BIG, STRONG, SILENT TYPE?

TRY THIS ONE!

Most people think of Dodge as a medium-price car. Because it's big. Almost 18 ft. long.

But in spite of bigness or tradition, or what you may think, the 1963 Dodge is a low-price automobile.

For instance, if you can afford a Chevy, you can afford a Dodge.

We are not talking about one special model. There are 24 models, in three series, all in the low-price field.

And Dodge is an automobile so well-built it is backed by a five year or 50,000 mile warranty*.

No wonder we call them "The Dependables". They are.

*Your Dodge Dealer's Warranty against defects in material and workmanship on 1963 cars has been expanded to include parts replacement or repair without charge for required parts or labor for five years or 50,000 miles, whichever comes first; on the engine block, head and internal parts: (excluding manual clutch): torque converter, drive shaft, universal joints (excluding dust covers), rear axle and differential, and rear wheel bearings—provided the vehicle has been serviced at reasonable intervals according to the Dodge Certified Car Care schedules.

THE LOW PRICE
1963 DODGE!!!

DODGE DIVISION ✦ CHRYSLER MOTORS CORPORATION

1963 AUBURN AND ALABAMA

COLLEGE FOOTBALL GAME

Alabama takes on the Auburn Tigers at Birmingham and the Crimson Tide is up against a Tiger of a different stripe this year.

Auburn's **Mailon Kent** gets off a pass to **Bucky Wade** for 12 yards.

Auburn hasn't beaten Alabama in five years, but plays like this 7-yard pickup by **Tucker Frederickson** are writing a different story this year.

It's set up for **Woody Woodall** and his field goal is good to put Auburn in front, 3-0.

With a 30-mile-an-hour wind at his back, **John Kilgore** boots one down to the Alabama 5-yard line.

Benny Nelson is waiting for the ball, but he's tripped up and Auburn's Kent recovers.

WHAT A YEAR IT WAS!

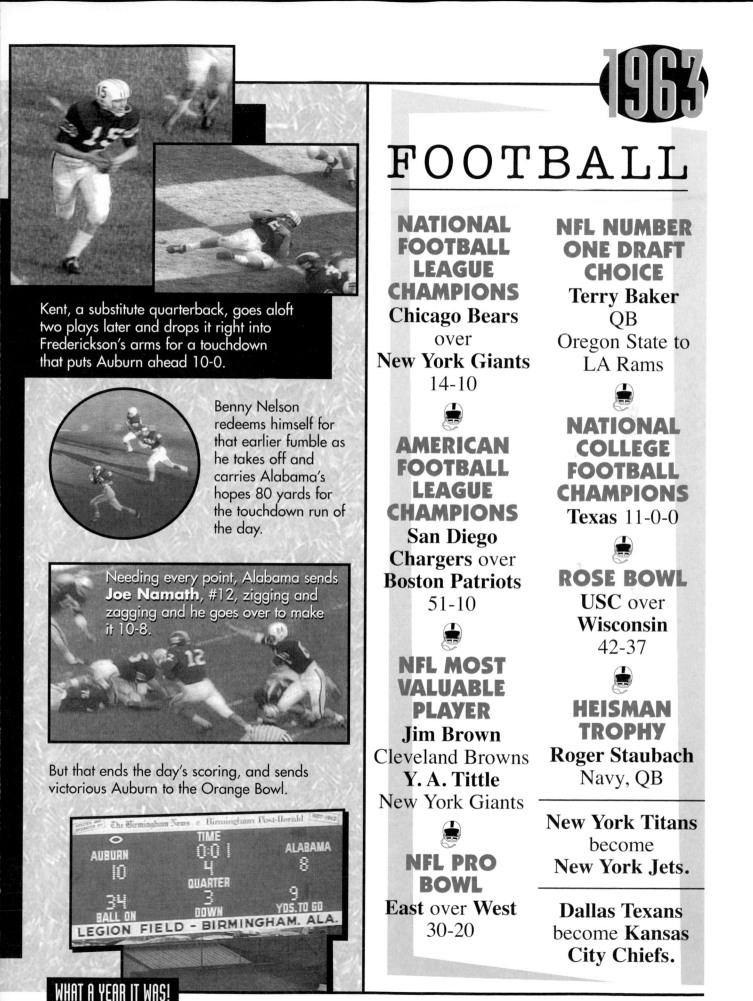

Kent, a substitute quarterback, goes aloft two plays later and drops it right into Frederickson's arms for a touchdown that puts Auburn ahead 10-0.

Benny Nelson redeems himself for that earlier fumble as he takes off and carries Alabama's hopes 80 yards for the touchdown run of the day.

Needing every point, Alabama sends **Joe Namath**, #12, zigging and zagging and he goes over to make it 10-8.

But that ends the day's scoring, and sends victorious Auburn to the Orange Bowl.

The Birmingham News & Birmingham Post-Herald 1927-1963

AUBURN	TIME 0:01	ALABAMA
10	4	8
	QUARTER	
34	3	9
BALL ON	DOWN	YDS. TO GO

LEGION FIELD - BIRMINGHAM, ALA.

WHAT A YEAR IT WAS!

FOOTBALL

NATIONAL FOOTBALL LEAGUE CHAMPIONS
Chicago Bears over **New York Giants** 14-10

AMERICAN FOOTBALL LEAGUE CHAMPIONS
San Diego Chargers over **Boston Patriots** 51-10

NFL MOST VALUABLE PLAYER
Jim Brown Cleveland Browns
Y. A. Tittle New York Giants

NFL PRO BOWL
East over **West** 30-20

NFL NUMBER ONE DRAFT CHOICE
Terry Baker QB Oregon State to LA Rams

NATIONAL COLLEGE FOOTBALL CHAMPIONS
Texas 11-0-0

ROSE BOWL
USC over **Wisconsin** 42-37

HEISMAN TROPHY
Roger Staubach Navy, QB

New York Titans become **New York Jets.**

Dallas Texans become **Kansas City Chiefs.**

FOOTBALL NEWS

The first 17 charter members are inducted into the new National Professional Football Hall of Fame in Canton, Ohio including the late **Bert Bell**, **Red Grange**, **Mel Hein**, **Cal Hubbard** and the late **Jim Thorpe**.

NFL's N.Y. Giants trade **Roosevelt (Rosey) Grier** to the Los Angeles Rams for **John LoVetere**.

Following **President Kennedy's** assassination, at the request of his family, the Army-Navy football game is postponed for one day.

Al **Davis** is new head coach and general manager of the Oakland Raiders and is later named AFL Coach of the Year by an AP poll of sportswriters.

The National Football League is shaken up by a betting scandal which results in **Pete Rozelle** suspending two of its star players – **Paul Hornung** of the Green Bay Packers and **Alex Karras** of the Detroit Lions.

Pete Rozelle, National Football Commissioner, is chosen "Sportsman of the Year" by SPORTS ILLUSTRATED.

In the second highest amount awarded in a U.S. libel action, **Wallace (Wally) Butts**, ex-University of Georgia athletic director, is awarded $3 million by a federal grand jury in Atlanta in his suit against the Curtis Publishing Co., publishers of the SATURDAY EVENING POST, who charged that the Alabama-Georgia football game had been rigged. On appeal the award is decreased to $460,000.

BASKETBALL

NBA CHAMPIONS

Boston Celtics
over
LA Lakers
4-2

•

NBA MOST VALUABLE PLAYER

BILL RUSSELL
Boston Celtics

•

NBA ALL-STAR GAME

East
over
West
MVP - BILL RUSSELL
Boston Celtics

•

NCAA CHAMPIONS

Loyola (Illinois)
over
Cincinnati
60-58
(overtime)

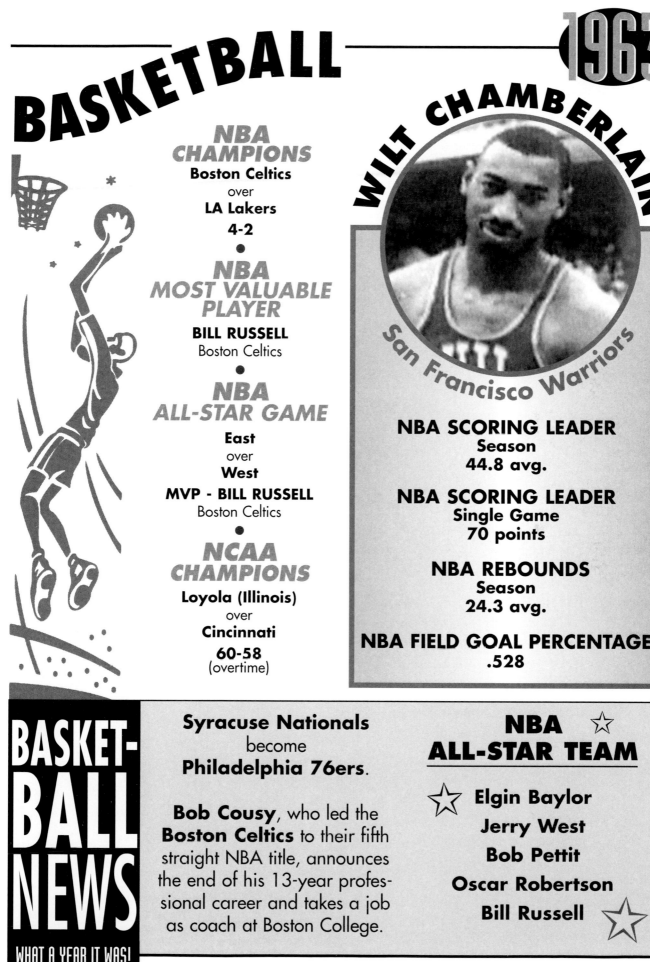

WILT CHAMBERLAIN
San Francisco Warriors

NBA SCORING LEADER
Season
44.8 avg.

NBA SCORING LEADER
Single Game
70 points

NBA REBOUNDS
Season
24.3 avg.

NBA FIELD GOAL PERCENTAGE
.528

BASKET-BALL NEWS

WHAT A YEAR IT WAS!

Syracuse Nationals become **Philadelphia 76ers.**

Bob Cousy, who led the **Boston Celtics** to their fifth straight NBA title, announces the end of his 13-year professional career and takes a job as coach at Boston College.

NBA ALL-STAR TEAM

Elgin Baylor
Jerry West
Bob Pettit
Oscar Robertson
Bill Russell

Basketball

The 13th annual basketball All-Star game - East vs. West - sees the East jumping to an early lead and the West spending its time trying to catch up.

Walt Bellamy, *#8, scores for the West, but the East bounces right back and that's the story throughout the game.*

The East's teamwork is superb.

There are 14,000 fans on hand, including celebrities like **Doris Day** and **Pat Boone**.

All-Star Game

Nearing the end of the first half, the West scores on some beautiful maneuvering.

Johnny Green, #11, does a yeoman's job for the East to keep them ahead offensively.

*The crowd watches every move of the West's favorite son, **Elgin Baylor**. He's held to 17 points tonight, but the East can't hold him as he passes to **Wilt Chamberlain** for a West score.*

The fans show their approval.

Johnny Green has the ball again. He misses the shot, but one of his teammates is right there to take over and the fans love it.

With less than 5 minutes to play, the West makes its final run led by Walt Bellamy.

*Leading the West by 8 points, the East moves out of danger as **Bill Russell** hooks one after another, and for the first time since 1960, the East wins the NBA All-Star game. They go into the game as underdogs but come out on top, 115 to 108.*

golf

GOLF NEWS

Jack Nicklaus

U.S. OPEN	Julius Boros Mary Mills
PGA/LPGA	Jack Nicklaus Mickey Wright
PGA/LPGA LEADING MONEY WINNER	Arnold Palmer $128,230 Mickey Wright $31,269
PGA PLAYER OF THE YEAR	Julius Boros
MASTERS	Jack Nicklaus
U.S. AMATEUR	Deane Beman Anne Quast Welts
BRITISH OPEN	Bob Charles
SENIOR PGA	Herman Barron

JACK NICKLAUS wins his first Masters Tournament and goes on to win the PGA championship and the World Series of Golf against ARNOLD PALMER and U.S. Open champion JULIUS BOROS.

•

JACK NICKLAUS and ARNOLD PALMER are the first professional golfers to ever win over $100,000, with Palmer being the top money winner for the fourth time in six years.

•

MICKEY WRIGHT is the first woman to win 11 major tournaments in a single year.

BOXING  NEWS

Cassius Clay (white trunks) challenges eastern heavyweight champ Gary Harrish in 1960's 33rd Inner City Golden Gloves match.

29-year-old ex-world featherweight champion **Davey Moore** dies of brain injuries he sustains in a title bout with **Sugar Ramos** in a 10-round knockout in Los Angeles. His death spurs renewed demands for the abolition of boxing, with Governor **Edmund G. Brown** calling for the end of boxing in California.

Just as he predicted, **Cassius Clay** KO's **Henry Cooper** in the fifth round in a match held in London.

Sonny Liston retains his heavyweight crown, knocking out **Floyd Patterson** in the first round.

THE RING MAGAZINE
FIGHT OF THE YEAR

Cassius Clay over
Doug Jones

THE RING MAGAZINE
FIGHTER OF THE YEAR

Cassius Clay

☞ **HEAVYWEIGHT**
SONNY LISTON

☞ **MIDDLEWEIGHT**
PAUL PENDER
DICK TIGER
JOEY GIARDELLO

☞ **WELTERWEIGHT**
EMILE GRIFFITH
LUIS RODRIGUEZ

☞ **FEATHERWEIGHT**
DAVEY MOORE
ULTIMINIO "SUGAR" RAMOS

☞ **LIGHTWEIGHT**
CARLOS ORTIZ

☞ **LIGHT HEAVYWEIGHT**
HAROLD JOHNSON
WILLIE PASTRANO

1963
Sugar Ray Robinson

Sugar Ray Robinson opens his European tour with a bout in Brussels as he takes on Belgian middleweight **Emile Sarens**.

Robinson is 43 years old, an age when most boxers are content to spend the day in a rocking chair looking over their newspaper clippings.

ROUND
6

In the sixth round Sarens has Robinson on the ropes and gives him a terrific punching, but, the warrior that he is, Robinson takes everything the Belgian champ can give.

WHAT A YEAR IT WAS!

Brussels Fight

The old master fights himself out of the tight corner.

In the seventh round, Robinson seems to get his second wind. This is Robinson's 167th fight. He was five-time middleweight champion.

ROUND 8

In the eighth round payoff, Robinson knocks out Sarens with a terrific punch to the body.

Robinson is still aiming to win back his middleweight title.

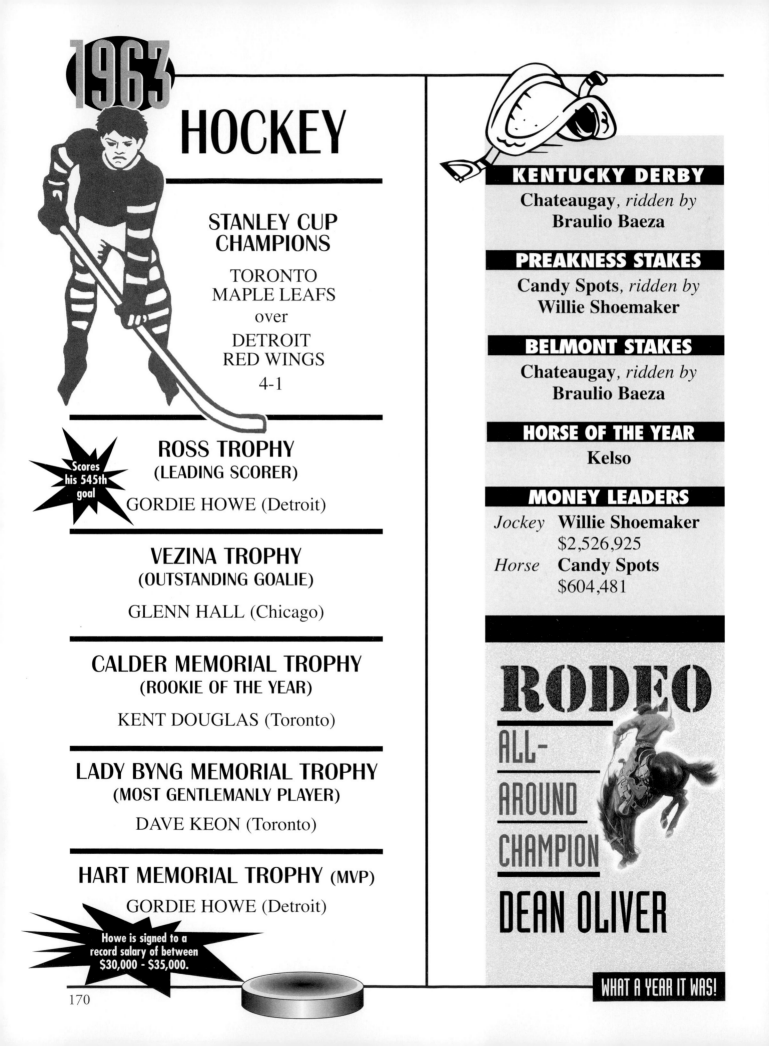

1963

HOCKEY

STANLEY CUP CHAMPIONS

TORONTO
MAPLE LEAFS
over
DETROIT
RED WINGS
4-1

ROSS TROPHY
(LEADING SCORER)

GORDIE HOWE (Detroit)

Scores his 545th goal

VEZINA TROPHY
(OUTSTANDING GOALIE)

GLENN HALL (Chicago)

CALDER MEMORIAL TROPHY
(ROOKIE OF THE YEAR)

KENT DOUGLAS (Toronto)

LADY BYNG MEMORIAL TROPHY
(MOST GENTLEMANLY PLAYER)

DAVE KEON (Toronto)

HART MEMORIAL TROPHY (MVP)

GORDIE HOWE (Detroit)

Howe is signed to a record salary of between $30,000 - $35,000.

170

KENTUCKY DERBY
Chateaugay, *ridden by*
Braulio Baeza

PREAKNESS STAKES
Candy Spots, *ridden by*
Willie Shoemaker

BELMONT STAKES
Chateaugay, *ridden by*
Braulio Baeza

HORSE OF THE YEAR
Kelso

MONEY LEADERS
Jockey **Willie Shoemaker**
$2,526,925
Horse **Candy Spots**
$604,481

RODEO
ALL-AROUND CHAMPION
DEAN OLIVER

TENNIS

U.S. OPEN

RAFAEL OSUNA over FRANK FROEHLING

MARIA BUENO over MARGARET SMITH

WIMBLEDON

CHUCK McKINLEY over FRED STOLLE

MARGARET SMITH over BILLIE JEAN MOFFITT

DAVIS CUP

USA over Australia, 3-2

U.S. PRO TENNIS TITLE

KEN ROSEWALL

20-year-old **Arthur Ashe** of Richmond, Virginia becomes America's first black player to be named to the Davis Cup team.

Figure Skating

World Champions

DONALD McPHERSON
Canada

SJOUKJE DIJKSTRA
Holland

U.S. Champions

THOMAS LITZ

LORRAINE HANLON

CAR RACING

INDIANAPOLIS 500

Parnelli Jones
Agajanian-Willard Special, 143.137 mph

LE MANS

Lodovico Scarfiotti & Lorenzo Bandini
Ferrari 250, 118.08 mph

WINSTON CUP

Joe Weatherly

CRAIG BREEDLOVE sets world land speed record at 407.45 mph in his 35-foot jet-powered *Spirit of America*, making him the first U.S. racer in 35 years to hold the land speed record.

WHAT A YEAR IT WAS!

1963

BOWLING

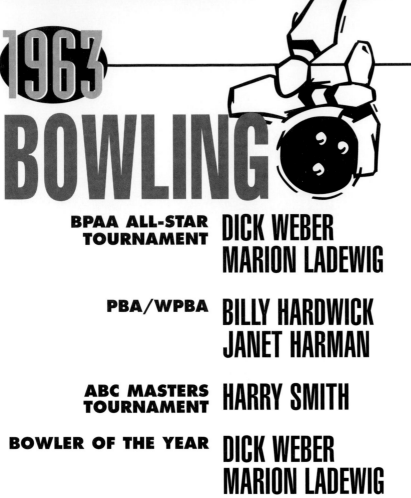

BPAA ALL-STAR TOURNAMENT	**DICK WEBER** **MARION LADEWIG**
PBA/WPBA	**BILLY HARDWICK** **JANET HARMAN**
ABC MASTERS TOURNAMENT	**HARRY SMITH**
BOWLER OF THE YEAR	**DICK WEBER** **MARION LADEWIG**

Despite the American Bowling Congress position that the so-called "livelier" pins won't affect individual scores, some professional bowlers disagree and feel it will allow the average bowler to achieve higher scores.

CHESS

WORLD CHAMPIONS
Mikhail Botvinnik (U.S.S.R.)
Tigran Petrosian (U.S.S.R.)

U.S. CHAMPION
Bobby Fischer

• • •

25-year-old **William Lombardy** of New York wins the U.S. Open championship in Chicago and 16-year-old **Kate Sillars** of Wilmette, Illinois wins the women's title.

TRACK & FIELD

BOSTON MARATHON
Aurele Vandendriessche, Belgium

U.S.S.R.'s **VALERY BRUMEL** sets a new world high-jump record of 7 feet, 5 3/4 inches in Moscow during a U.S.-Soviet track meet.

American **HENRY CARR** runs 200 meters in a record 0:20.3.

In St. Louis, **BOB HAYES** sets record in 100-yard dash, 9.1 sec.

Vaulter **JOHN PENNEL** of Northeast Louisiana State College sets a world record of 17 feet, 3/4 inch.

WHAT A YEAR IT WAS!

CYCLING

TOUR de FRANCE

Jacques Anquetil
France

Dog Show Winner
••••••••••••••••••
WESTMINSTER KENNEL CLUB
Best in Show

Wakefield's Black Knight
English Springer Spaniel

POCKET BILLIARDS WORLD CHAMPION

Luther Lassiter
Elizabeth City, North Carolina

famous BIRTHS

Charles Barkley
A. C. Green
Randy Johnson
Michael Jordan
Karl Malone
Mark McGwire
Hakeem Olajuwon

PASSINGS

Ernie Davis (23)

Rogers "Rajah" Hornsby (66)

ASSORTED AWARDS ①

AP ATHLETE OF THE YEAR
Sandy Koufax (Baseball)
Mickey Wright (Golf)

THE HICKOK BELT
Sandy Koufax (Baseball)

WHAT A YEAR IT WAS!

1963 WAS A GREAT YEAR, BUT...

THE BEST IS YET TO COME!